W9-BTM-696

Quick to Stitch
Cross Stitch Cards

D&C

David and Charles

A DAVID & CHARLES BOOK
Copyright © David & Charles Limited 2006

David & Charles is an F+W Publications Inc. company
4700 East Galbraith Road
Cincinnati, OH 45236

First published in the UK in 2006

Designs copyright © Claire Crompton, Joan Elliott,
Joanne Sanderson and Lesley Teare 2006
Text, photography and layout copyright © David & Charles 2006

Claire Crompton, Joan Elliott, Joanne Sanderson and Lesley Teare
have asserted their right to be identified as authors of this work in
accordance with the Copyright, Designs and Patents Act, 1988.

All rights reserved. No part of this publication may be reproduced,
stored in a retrieval system, or transmitted, in any form or by any
means, electronic or mechanical, by photocopying, recording or
otherwise, without prior permission in writing from the publisher.

The designs in this book are copyright and must not be stitched
for resale.

A catalogue record for this book is available from the British Library.

ISBN-13: 978-0-7153-2245-1 hardback
ISBN-10: 0-7153-2245-1 hardback

ISBN-13: 978-0-7153-2505-6 paperback
ISBN-10: 0-7153-2505-1 paperback

Printed in China by SNP Leefung
for David & Charles
Brunel House   Newton Abbot   Devon

Executive commissioning editor Cheryl Brown
Editor Jennifer Proverbs
Head of design Prudence Rogers
Designer Jodie Lystor
Project editor and chart preparation Linda Clements
Photographers Karl Adamson and Kim Sayer
Production controller Ros Napper

Visit our website at www.davidandcharles.co.uk

David & Charles books are available from all good bookshops;
alternatively you can contact our Orderline on 0870 9908222 or
write to us at FREEPOST EX2 110, D&C Direct, Newton Abbot,
TQ12 4ZZ (no stamp required UK only); US customers call
800-289-0963 and Canadian customers call 800-840-5220.

Contents

Let's celebrate 34

Days to remember 62

Introduction

There are so many occasions throughout our lives that are made even more memorable by the giving of a card – and what better card to give than one hand stitched with love? But we often run out of time in our busy lives for this personal touch and so miss the chance to create a keepsake treasured by the recipient. Well, no more: this book will help you find the right card for the right occasion and cross stitch the designs quickly and easily.

Cross stitch and cards are the perfect combination. We get the opportunity to embroider a design we've chosen especially for the recipient, to add words of greeting, friendship, love, congratulation or comfort and package it all up in an attractive card they can keep forever. We can even embellish a card or gift tag to make it more personal and special.

Occasions for card giving seem to increase all the time so this collection aims to provide you with cross stitch designs that can not only be stitched quickly but also offer varying and distinctive styles – there are sentimental cards, cute cards, quirky cards and traditional cards, as you can see from some of the examples below.

In the first chapter there are designs for birthdays for all ages, from new-born to nonagenarian. This is followed by a range of cards perfect for offering congratulations – new baby, new job, new home, you name it. The final chapter offers designs for special celebrations, those annual events we enjoy so much, such as Christmas and Easter.

At the end of the book are sections on the materials and techniques you will need, including how to work the stitches. This is followed by lots of advice on using cards (page 96) and how to make your own cards and tags (page 98). Of course, you could also use the designs for other items, such as small framed pictures,

drawstring bags and embroidered patches to decorate book covers. There is also a selection of charted alphabets on page 102 to help you customize your cross stitch and add personal messages.

A key feature of this book is that the designs have been graded according to the time they take to complete, so look out for the following icons:

Quick These card projects have the most detail but you should still be able to complete the cross stitch design in a weekend.

Quicker These designs require less stitching and usually have fewer colours, so should only take a day to complete.

Quickest These are the easiest designs, taking only about an evening to stitch – perfect for when time is short.

The Quick Stitch panel opposite will help to get you started. So, pick an occasion and begin stitching or just dip into the designs and choose your favourites – either way you'll soon be creating lovely cross stitch cards, quickly.

Quick Stitch

This panel is a quick-start reminder of the basic supplies and instructions you need to create the cross stitch cards in this book. See also Quick Cards on page 101 for tips on producing cards quickly and easily.

You will need
- Embroidery fabric bigger than the finished design size
- Tapestry needle size 24–26
- Embroidery threads as listed in the chart key
- Single-fold card or tag or double-fold card with aperture, to fit your embroidery
- Double-sided adhesive tape
- Trims or embellishments as desired

Get ready. . . Find and mark the centre of your fabric (see page 93) and then locate the centre of the chart by following the arrows at the chart sides. Stitch from the centre outwards.

Start stitching. . . Stitch over one block of Aida (or two threads of evenweave). Use two strands of thread for full and three-quarter cross stitches and French knots, and one strand for backstitches and long stitches, unless otherwise instructed. See page 94 for working the stitches. Attach beads with a beading needle (see page 95).

Finish off. . . Refer to pages 96–97 for how to mount your completed embroidery – on a single-fold card, or in a double-fold card, or on a tag. Add trims and embellishments to your card as desired – see page 100 for ideas.

CHOOSING A CARD
You may want to use ready-made card mounts, like most of the projects in this book (see page 96 and list of suppliers on page 103) or prefer to make your own cards (see page 98), but in either case you should check that your embroidery will fit on to the card or into the window aperture. Measure the aperture and compare this to the finished design size of the cross stitch (given with each project). The embroidery needs to fit comfortably within the aperture, with sufficient fabric behind the aperture for strips of double-sided tape.

Birthday wishes

There are some wonderful cards in this section that are perfect quick-stitch designs for all sorts of birthdays; from sweet new-born babies, to street-smart teenagers and on to those more 'mature' milestones. There are cards here for everyone – for the dearest of friends, for dog and cat lovers, for toy-mad toddlers, for fanatic gardeners and for those growing old disgracefully.

Choose a 'quick' project for a weekend of happy stitching, or create a card in less time by choosing the 'quicker' or 'quickest' designs. The cards each have a distinctive look: sometimes pretty and romantic, sometimes humorous and quirky, but always easy and rewarding to stitch – the choice is yours.

Love Me, Love My Dog   Designs by Claire Crompton

Quick

Finished design size on 16-count 8 x 11cm (3⅛ x 4⅜in)

Canine Party

When it's a dog-lover's birthday, dogs are sometimes more important guests than people!

You Will Need
- 18 x 21cm (7 x 8¼in) 16-count white Aida
- Double-fold card to fit embroidery

Stitch and make up your card – see Quick Stitch, page 5. To embellish, draw pink paw prints on the card mount.

Who's Present?

Some dogs don't let anything distract them from the important things in life!

You Will Need
- 16.5 x 19cm (6½ x 7½in) 14-count white Aida
- Double-fold card to fit embroidery

Stitch and make up your card – see Quick Stitch, page 5.

Quicker

Finished design size on 14-count 6.3 x 9cm (2½ x 3½in)

Quickest

You're Grrrreat!

This cheeky mutt makes a cute quick-stitch gift tag or small card for someone mad about dogs. The sparkly bead collar is a nice finishing touch.

You Will Need
- 10 x 9cm (4 x 3½in) 14-count white Aida
- Mill Hill glass seed beads 02010 silver
- Dark mauve card for tag

Follow Quick Stitch, page 5 and make a tag (page 98).

Finished design size on 14-count 5 x 3.6cm (2 x 1½in)

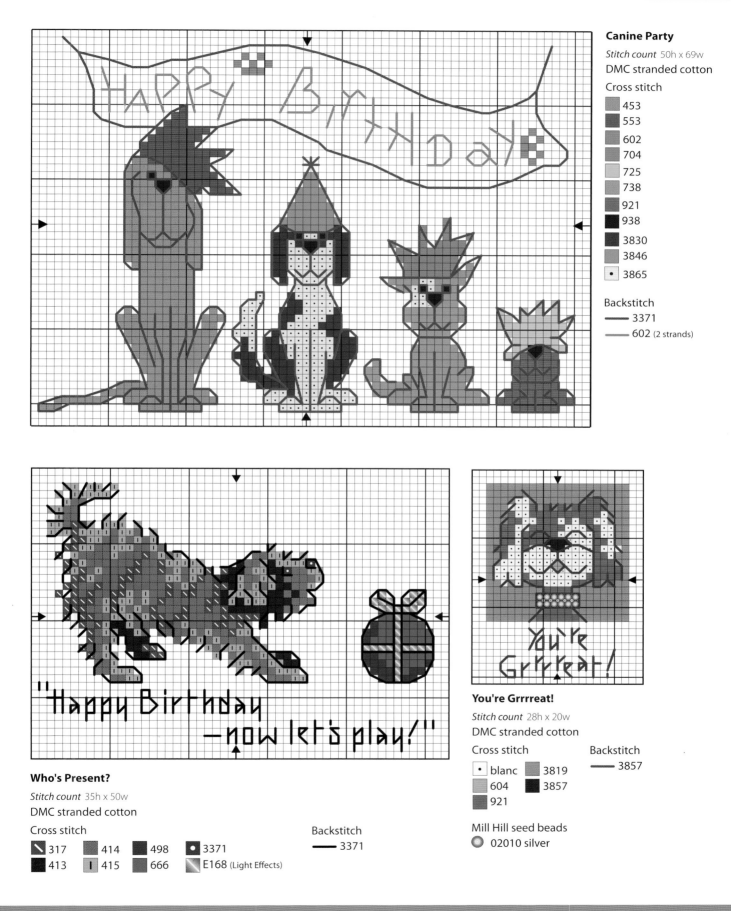

Canine Party

Stitch count 50h x 69w

DMC stranded cotton

Cross stitch

	453
	553
	602
	704
	725
	738
	921
	938
	3830
	3846
•	3865

Backstitch

—— 3371

—— 602 (2 strands)

Who's Present?

Stitch count 35h x 50w

DMC stranded cotton

Cross stitch

◣ 317		414		498	◉ 3371
413	I	415		666	◪ E168 (Light Effects)

Backstitch

—— 3371

You're Grrrreat!

Stitch count 28h x 20w

DMC stranded cotton

Cross stitch

•	blanc		3819
	604		3857
	921		

Backstitch

—— 3857

Mill Hill seed beads

◯ 02010 silver

Purrfect Birthday Designs by Claire Crompton

Quick

Finished design size on 14-count 8.7 x 12.7cm (3½ x 5in)

A Perfect Picture

This would have been the perfect message but someone is more interested in a butterfly than a birthday!

You Will Need
- 19 x 23.5cm (7½ x 9¼in) 14-count cream Aida
- Double-fold card to fit embroidery

Stitch and make up your card – see Quick Stitch, page 5.

Quicker

Cats Spell It Out

Let these cute cats say 'Happy Birthday' to the cat-lover in your life.

You Will Need
- 14 x 21.5cm (5⅝ x 8⅝in) 14-count white Aida
- Single-fold card to fit embroidery
- Heavyweight iron-on interfacing

Stitch and make up your card – see Quick Stitch, page 5. Mount the embroidery after backing with iron-on interfacing (see page 97). Draw paw prints on the card mount.

Finished design size on 14-count 4 x 11.5cm (1½ x 4½in)

Quickest

Finished design size on 14-count
5 x 4.3cm (2 x 1¾in)

The Cat's Whiskers!

Make a loved one feel like the cat that got the cream.

You Will Need
- 10.5 x 9.5cm (4⅛ x 3¾in) 14-count white Aida
- One Mill Hill glass seed bead 02010 silver
- Two 15cm (6in) lengths of thin silver craft wire for whiskers
- Gift tag to fit embroidery

Follow Quick Stitch, page 5. Thread a wire from the front at one side of the face to the back and out at the front on the other side. Repeat with the second wire. Cover the back of the wires with tape. Curl each wire over a pen and then trim. Mount on the tag.

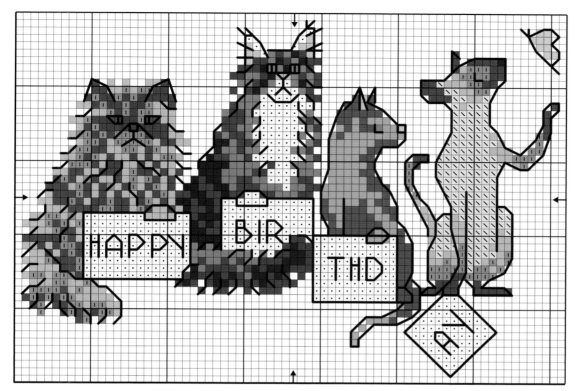

A Perfect Picture

Stitch count 48h x 70w

DMC stranded cotton

Cross stitch

402	436	799	928
434	761	I 927	938

989	3776	• blanc
3768	\ 3865	

Backstitch
— 3371

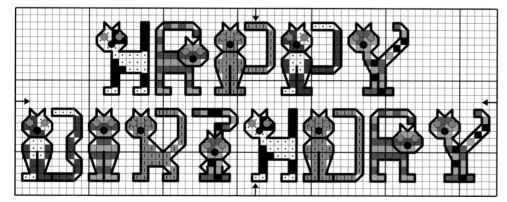

Cats Spell It Out

Stitch count 22h x 63w

DMC stranded cotton

Cross stitch

310	921
402	I 927
433	• blanc
435	

Backstitch
— 3371

French knots
● 310
● 989

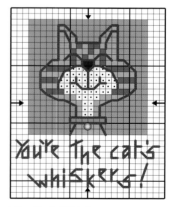
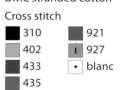

The Cat's Whiskers

Stitch count 29h x 24w

DMC stranded cotton

Cross stitch

704	3846	• blanc
893	3854	
900	3857	

Backstitch
— 3857

Mill Hill seed bead
◎ 02010 silver

Celebrate Friendship Designs by Joan Elliott

Finished design size on 18-count 9 x 9cm (3½ x 3½in)

Friends are Flowers

A card like this is the perfect way to let a friend know how special they are.

You Will Need
- 24 x 24cm (9½ x 9½in) 18-count antique white Aida
- Double-fold card to fit embroidery
- Narrow ribbon to trim

Stitch and make up your card – see Quick Stitch, page 5.

Quicker

Finished design size on 14-count 6.7 x 6.7cm (2½ x 2½in)

Forever Friends

This versatile design could be a birthday card, to thank a friend for their company or even to say sorry.

You Will Need
- 19 x 19cm (7½ x 7½in) 14-count antique white Aida
- Double-fold card to fit embroidery • Narrow ribbon to trim

Stitch and make up your card – see Quick Stitch, page 5.

Quickest

Friendship Treasured

Even a simple card can tell a friend they are a treasured part of your life, especially on their birthday.

You Will Need
- 17.8 x 17.8cm (7 x 7in) 14-count antique white Aida
- Double-fold card to fit embroidery
- Narrow ribbon to trim

Stitch and make up your tag – see Quick Stitch, page 5.

Finished design size on 14-count 4.5 x 4.5cm (1¾ x 1¾in)

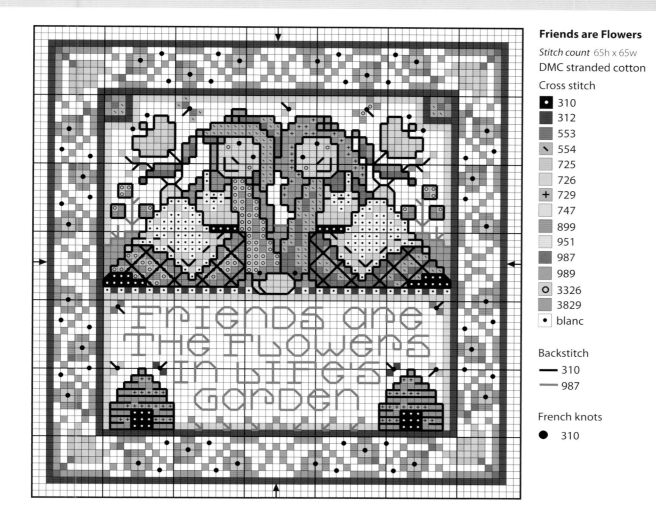

Friends are Flowers

Stitch count 65h x 65w

DMC stranded cotton

Cross stitch

◼	310
	312
	553
◤	554
	725
	726
+	729
	747
	899
	951
	987
	989
○	3326
	3829
•	blanc

Backstitch

— 310

— 987

French knots

● 310

Forever Friends

Stitch count 37h x 37w

DMC stranded cotton

Cross stitch

◼	310
	725
	899
	987
	989
○	3326
	3829
•	blanc

Backstitch

— 310

French knots

● 310

Friendship Treasured

Stitch count 25h x 25w

DMC stranded cotton

Cross stitch

	312		987
	747		989
	899	○	3326
	951	•	blanc

Backstitch

— 310

— 987

Celtic Greetings For Him   Designs by Joan Elliott

Quick

Celtic Good Fortune

Share words of encouragement and wishes of good
fortune with the special person in your life.

You Will Need
- 24 x 24cm (9½ x 9½in)
  18-count white Aida
- Double-fold card to fit embroidery
- Narrow ribbon to trim

Stitch and make up your card –
see Quick Stitch, page 5.

Finished design size on 18-count 9 x 9cm (3½ x 3½in)

Quicker

Finished design size on 14-count 6.7 x 6.7cm (2½ x 2½in)

Celtic Knot

Blue and gold make a striking combination
in this elegant design.

You Will Need
- 19 x 19cm (7½ x 7½in) 14-count white Aida
- Double-fold card to fit embroidery
- Narrow ribbon to trim

Stitch and make up your card –
see Quick Stitch, page 5.

Celtic Cross

This simple but attractive cross would make a
perfect greeting at a seasonal time of year.

Quickest

You Will Need
- 17.8 x 17.8cm (7 x 7in) 14-count white Aida
- Double-fold card/tag to fit embroidery
- Narrow ribbon to trim

Stitch and make up your tag –
see Quick Stitch, page 5.

*Finished design size
on 14-count*
4.5 x 4.5cm (1¾ x 1¾in)

Celtic Good Fortune

Stitch count 65h x 65w

DMC stranded cotton

Cross stitch

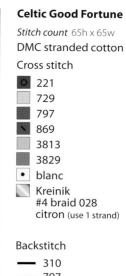

⊚	221
	729
	797
◣	869
	3813
	3829
•	blanc
◹	Kreinik #4 braid 028 citron (use 1 strand)

Backstitch

— 310
— 797

Celtic Knot

Stitch count 37h x 37w

DMC stranded cotton

Cross stitch

⊡	310
	502
	729
◹	798
	799
◣	869
	975
	3813
✕	3826
	3829
◹	Kreinik #4 braid 028 citron (use 1 strand)

Backstitch

— 310

French knots

● 310
● 975

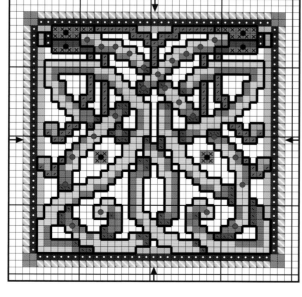

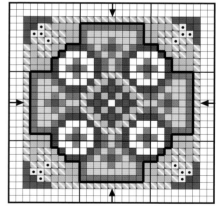

Celtic Cross

Stitch count 25h x 25w

DMC stranded cotton

Cross stitch

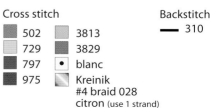

	502		3813
	729		3829
	797	•	blanc
	975	◹	Kreinik #4 braid 028 citron (use 1 strand)

Backstitch

— 310

Finished design size on 14-count 7 x 7.6cm (2¾ x 3in)

A Job Well Done

This birthday design will be perfect for the gardening enthusiast in your family.

You Will Need
- 15 x 15cm (6 x 6in) 14-count pale blue Aida
- Double-fold card to fit embroidery

Stitch and make up your card – see Quick Stitch, page 5.

Quicker

Finished design size on 14-count 7 x 3.7cm (2¾ x 1½in)

Sitting Pretty

This charming card could have the addition of a little bee or butterfly charm.

You Will Need
- 15 x 9cm (6 x 3½in) 14-count pale blue Aida
- Double-fold card to fit embroidery (Impress Cards)

Stitch and make up your card – see Quick Stitch, page 5.

Quickest

Showered with Love

This little motif makes a charming tag for a gardening gift.

You Will Need
- 10 x 10cm (4 x 4in) 14-count pale blue Aida
- Orange card for tag • Iron-on interfacing
- Ribbon or cord for tie

Follow Quick Stitch, page 5. Back the stitching with interfacing (page 97) and make a tag from orange card (see page 98).

Finished design size on 14-count 3 x 3.5cm (1¼ x 1⅜in)

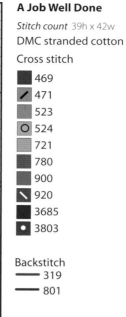

A Job Well Done

Stitch count 39h x 42w

DMC stranded cotton

Cross stitch

■	469
╱	471
■	523
○	524
■	721
■	780
■	900
╲	920
■	3685
●	3803

Backstitch
— 319
— 801

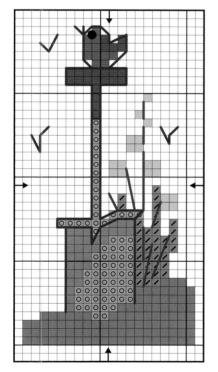

Sitting Pretty

Stitch count 38h x 20w

DMC stranded cotton

Cross stitch

╱	471
■	523
○	524
■	728
■	780
■	900
■	3829

Backstitch
— 319
— 801

French knot
● 310
(bird's eye)

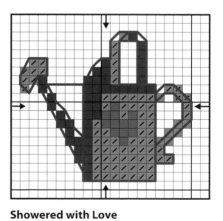

Showered with Love

Stitch count 17h x 19w

DMC stranded cotton

Cross stitch

■	469
╱	471
■	900

Backstitch
— 319

Oriental Greetings For Her   Designs by Joan Elliott

Peony and Dragonfly

The delicate peony blossom and the shimmer of a dragonfly carry words of joy on this lovely card.

You Will Need
- 24 x 24cm (9½ x 9½in) 18-count antique white Aida
- Double-fold card to fit embroidery
- Narrow ribbon to trim

Stitch and make up your card –
see Quick Stitch, page 5.

Finished design size on 18-count 9 x 9cm (3½ x 3½in)

Quicker

For Beauty

This beautiful, ultra feminine kimono carries the Chinese symbol for beauty.

You Will Need
- 19 x 19cm (7½ x 7½in) 14-count antique white Aida
- Double-fold card to fit embroidery   • Narrow ribbon to trim

Stitch and make up your card –
see Quick Stitch, page 5.

Finished design size on 14-count 6.7 x 6.7cm (2½ x 2½in)

Quickest

Oriental Wish

This small gift tag wishes the recipient double happiness.

You Will Need
- 17.8 x 17.8cm (7 x 7in) 14-count antique white Aida
- Double-fold card/tag to fit embroidery   • Narrow ribbon to trim

Stitch and make up your tag – see Quick Stitch, page 5.

*Finished design size
on 14-count*
4.5 x 4.5cm (1¾ x 1¾in)

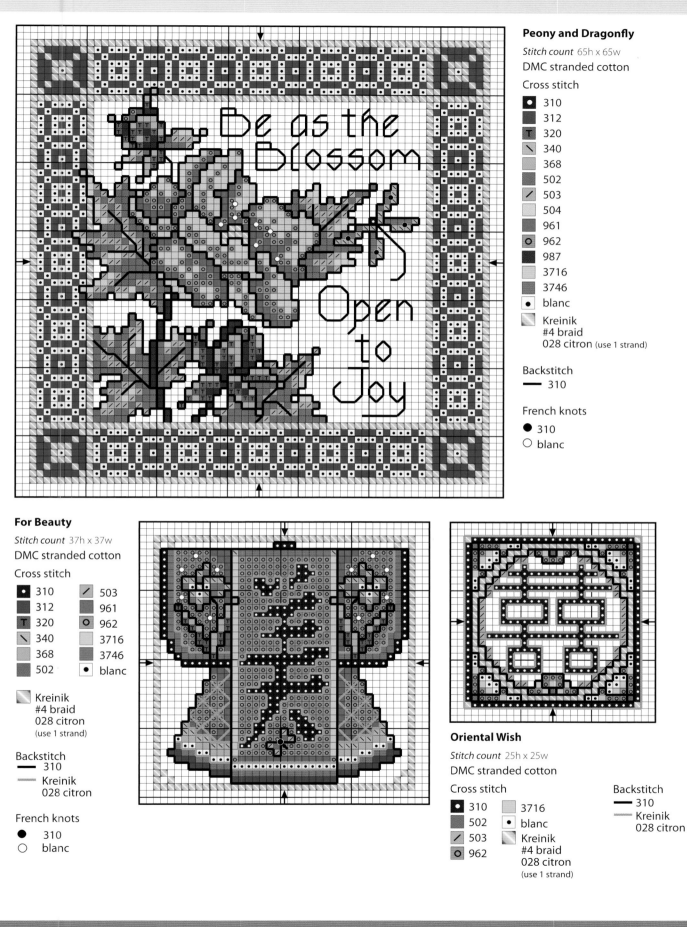

Peony and Dragonfly

Stitch count 65h x 65w

DMC stranded cotton

Cross stitch

◨	310
■	312
T	320
◺	340
▨	368
▦	502
◹	503
▨	504
▦	961
○	962
■	987
▨	3716
▨	3746
•	blanc
◸	Kreinik #4 braid 028 citron (use 1 strand)

Backstitch
— 310

French knots
● 310
○ blanc

For Beauty

Stitch count 37h x 37w

DMC stranded cotton

Cross stitch

◨	310		◹	503
■	312			961
T	320		○	962
◺	340			3716
▨	368		▦	3746
▦	502		•	blanc

◸ Kreinik #4 braid 028 citron (use 1 strand)

Backstitch
— 310
══ Kreinik 028 citron

French knots
● 310
○ blanc

Oriental Wish

Stitch count 25h x 25w

DMC stranded cotton

Cross stitch

◨	310		▨	3716
▦	502		•	blanc
◹	503		◸	Kreinik #4 braid 028 citron (use 1 strand)
○	962			

Backstitch
— 310
══ Kreinik 028 citron

Heaven Is A Garden   Designs by Lesley Teare

Quick

Finished design size on 14-count 9.5 x 5cm (3¾ x 2in)

Topiary Charm
You are sure to have a lovely weekend stitching this delightful design.

You Will Need
- 16.5 x 14cm (6½ x 5½in) 14-count pale green Aida
- Double-fold card to fit embroidery (Impress Cards)

Stitch and make up your card – see Quick Stitch, page 5.

Bee Happy
This charming design is simple to stitch but will still get your message across.

Quicker

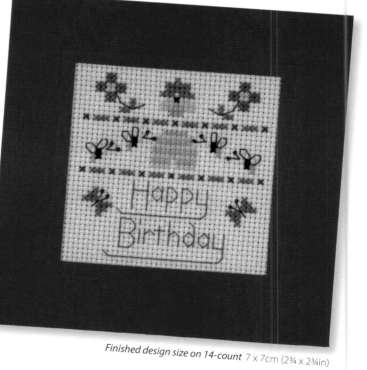

You Will Need
- 14 x 14cm (5½ x 5½in) 14-count white Aida
- Double-fold card to fit embroidery

Stitch and make up your card – see Quick Stitch, page 5.

Finished design size on 14-count 7 x 7cm (2¾ x 2¾in)

Quickest

Poppy Passion
This stylish, contemporary design features an ever-popular motif.

Finished design size on 14-count 3.5 x 3.3cm (1½ x 1⅜in)

You Will Need
- 10 x 10cm (4 x 4in) 14-count pale lime Aida
- Cream card for tag • Iron-on interfacing
- Red ribbon for tie

Follow Quick Stitch, page 5 and then make a tag (page 98) and mount the stitching.

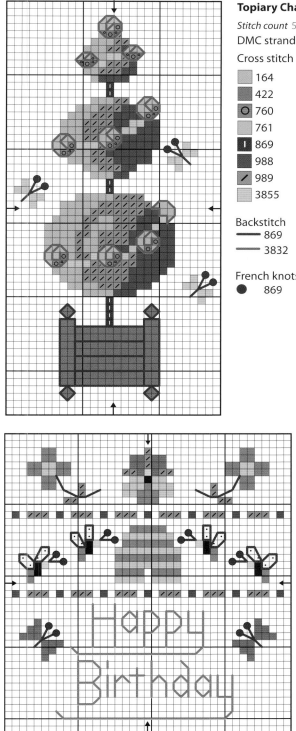
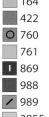

Topiary Charm

Stitch count 52h x 26w

DMC stranded cotton

Cross stitch

- 164
- 422
- ⊙ 760
- 761
- ❙ 869
- 988
- ╱ 989
- 3855

Backstitch
—— 869
—— 3832

French knots
● 869

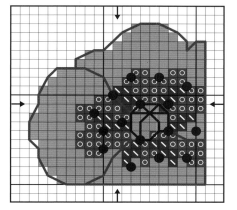

Poppy Passion

Stitch count 18h x 19w

DMC stranded cotton

Cross stitch	Backstitch	French knots
╲ 347	—— 310	● 310
⊙ 349	—— 347	
351		
3819		

Bee Happy

Stitch count 38h x 37w

DMC stranded cotton

Cross stitch

■ 310	792	3854
553	╱ 989	3855
745	3838	• blanc

Backstitch
—— 869
—— 3838

French knots
● 869

Baby Girl's 1st Birthday Designs by Joanne Sanderson

Finished design size on 14-count
7.4 x 6.3cm (3 x 2½in)

Quick

Birthday Kitten

Stitch this irresistible kitten in a weekend to celebrate a little girl's first birthday.

You Will Need
- 13cm x 13cm (5 x 5in) 14-count white Aida
- Dark pink piece of card, with aperture cut to fit embroidery
- Pink single-fold card 14 x 14cm (5½ x 5½in)

Stitch and make up your card – see Quick Stitch, page 5. Trim the embroidery to fit beneath the dark pink frame and stick with double-sided tape. Stick the mounted embroidery on the single-fold card.

Quicker

Message from Teddy

Stitch this cute bear for a lovely first birthday card. The number can be changed to suit any age – see chart on page 102.

You Will Need
- 18 x 13cm (7 x 5in) 14-count white Aida
- Double-fold card to fit embroidery • Ribbon to trim

Stitch and make up your card – see Quick Stitch, page 5. Embellish with a ribbon bow.

Finished design size on 14-count 6.3 x 5.8 cm (2½ x 2¼in)

One Today

Stitch this simple design as a gift tag or small birthday card.

Quickest

Finished design size on 14-count
2.4 x 2.9cm (1 x 1⅛in)

You Will Need
- 10 x 10cm (4 x 4in) 14-count pink Aida
- Piece of mid pink card 5.7 x 6.3cm (1¾ x 2in)
- Piece of light pink card 8 x 13cm (3 x 5in) folded in half
- Iron-on interfacing • Ribbon to trim

Follow Quick Stitch, page 5 but use three strands for cross stitch. Back the embroidery with iron-on interfacing (page 97) and then stick on the mid pink card. Mount on the light pink card and punch a hole for a bow.

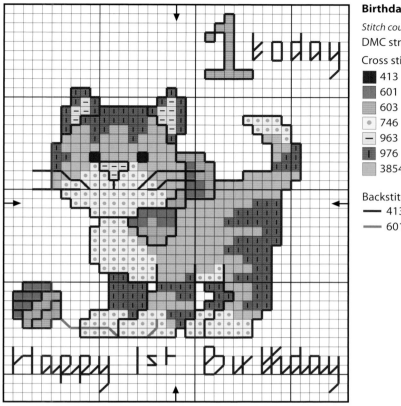

Birthday Kitten

Stitch count 41h x 34w

DMC stranded cotton

Cross stitch

- ■ 413
- ■ 601
- ▦ 603
- • 746
- – 963
- ▮ 976
- ▨ 3854

Backstitch

- — 413
- — 601

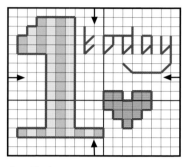

One Today

Stitch count 13h x 16w

DMC stranded cotton

Cross stitch

- ▢ 744
- ▨ 961
- ▨ 3716

Backstitch

- — 317

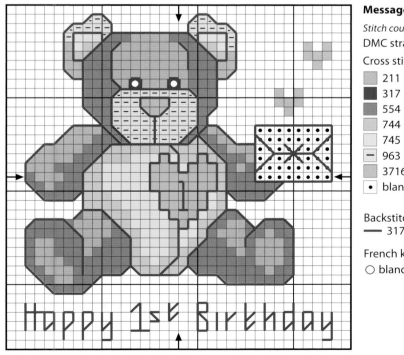

Message from Teddy

Stitch count 35h x 32w

DMC stranded cotton

Cross stitch

- ▦ 211
- ■ 317
- ▨ 554
- ▤ 744
- ▢ 745
- – 963
- ▨ 3716
- • blanc

Backstitch

- — 317

French knots

- ○ blanc

Baby Boy's 1st Birthday Designs by Joanne Sanderson

⏱ Quick

Toys Galore

Stitch this bright card in a weekend. Alternatively stitch the motifs separately for smaller cards and gift tags.

You Will Need
- 18cm x 13cm (7 x 5in) 14-count white Aida
- Double-fold card to fit embroidery

Stitch and make up your card –
see Quick Stitch, page 5.

Finished design size on 14-count 10.3 x 6cm (4 x 2³/₈in)

All Aboard the Birthday Train!

Stitch this bright little train design in a day.
The ribbon trim is an attractive addition.

⏱ Quicker

Finished design size on 14-count 4.7 x 6.5cm (1⁷/₈ x 2½in)

You Will Need
- 13 x 18cm (5 x 7in) 14-count white Aida
- Double-fold card to fit embroidery
- Ribbon to trim

Stitch and make up your card –
see Quick Stitch, page 5.

⏱ Quickest

Birthday Balloon

The backstitch thread on this bright balloon
is left long to look like the balloon's string.

You Will Need
- 10 x 10cm (4 x 4in) 14-count pale blue Aida
- Red card for tag • Iron-on interfacing • Ribbon to trim

Follow Quick Stitch, page 5 but use three strands for cross stitch.
After backstitching leave the thread to dangle. Make a tag (see page
98). Back the embroidery with iron-on interfacing (page 97)
and stick to the tag. Add a ribbon bow.

*Finished design size
on 14-count*
3.6 x 2.2cm (1½ x ⁷/₈in)

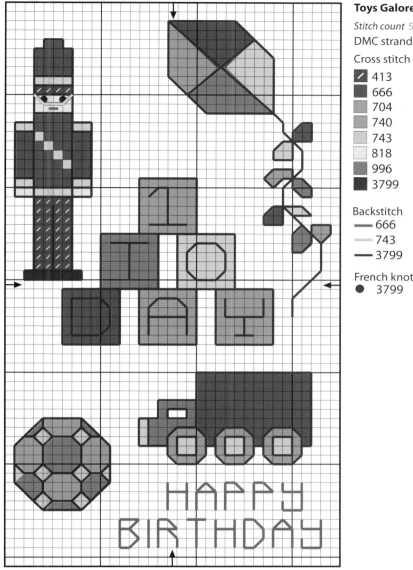

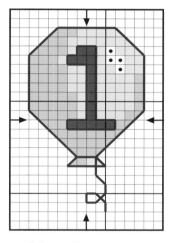

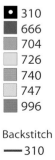

Toys Galore

Stitch count 57h x 33w

DMC stranded cotton

Cross stitch

- 413
- 666
- 704
- 740
- 743
- 818
- 996
- 3799

Backstitch

—— 666
—— 743
—— 3799

French knots

● 3799

Birthday Balloon

Stitch count 20h x 12w

DMC stranded cotton

Cross stitch (use 3 strands)   Backstitch

- 666   744   —— 310
- 742   ● blanc

All Aboard the Birthday Train

Stitch count 26h x 36w

DMC stranded cotton

Cross stitch

- 310
- 666
- 704
- 726
- 740
- 747
- 996

Backstitch

—— 310

Little Girls' Birthdays Are Magic! Designs by Joanne Sanderson

Quick

Fairy Birthday

This card is for little girls who like to dress up as fairies. Silver thread is perfect for fairy dust, with a ribbon bow to finish. The birthday number can be changed using the chart on page 102.

You Will Need
- 20 x 15cm (8 x 6in) 14-count white Aida
- Double-fold card to fit embroidery • Ribbon to trim

Stitch and make up your card – see Quick Stitch, page 5. Thread the ribbon through the Aida from front to back and to the front again, then tie in a bow. Mount the stitching into the card.

Finished design size on 14-count
10.9 x 6.9cm (4¼ x 2¾in)

Quicker

Finished design size on 14-count
8.5 x 5cm (3⅜ x 2in)

Pink Shoes

This pretty card would be suitable for girls of all ages. Change the birthday number using the chart on page 102.

You Will Need
- 18 x 13cm (7 x 5in) 14-count ivory Aida
- Double-fold card to fit embroidery

Stitch and make up your card – see Quick Stitch, page 5.

Quickest

A Gift for You

This versatile gift tag could be stitched using leftover threads and the colour scheme changed to suit a boy or even an adult.

You Will Need
- 10 x 10cm (4 x 4in) 14-count cream Aida
- Pink card for tag 15 x 10cm (6 x 4in)
- Iron-on interfacing • Organza ribbon to trim

Follow Quick Stitch, page 5. Make the tag (page 98). Back the embroidery with iron-on interfacing (page 97), trim and mount. Add the ribbon.

Finished design size on 14-count
3.4 x 3.3cm (1⅜ x 1¼in)

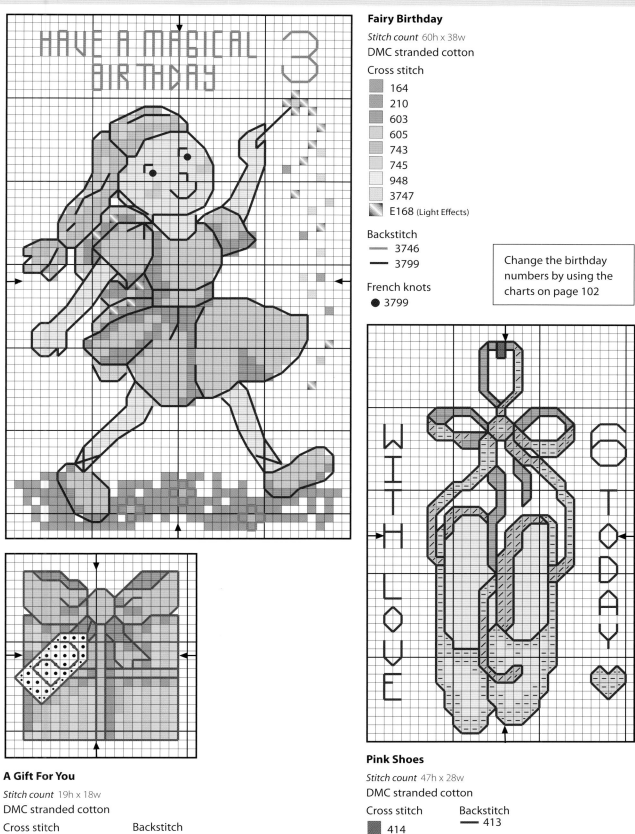

Fairy Birthday

Stitch count 60h x 38w

DMC stranded cotton

Cross stitch

	164
	210
	603
	605
	743
	745
	948
	3747
	E168 (Light Effects)

Backstitch

— 3746
— 3799

French knots

● 3799

Change the birthday numbers by using the charts on page 102

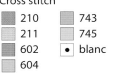

A Gift For You

Stitch count 19h x 18w

DMC stranded cotton

Cross stitch

	210		743
	211		745
	602	●	blanc
	604		

Backstitch

— 317

Pink Shoes

Stitch count 47h x 28w

DMC stranded cotton

Cross stitch

		Backstitch	
	414	—	413
	819		
	962		
—	963		
/	3716		

Little Boys' Birthdays Are Fun! Designs by Joanne Sanderson

Quick

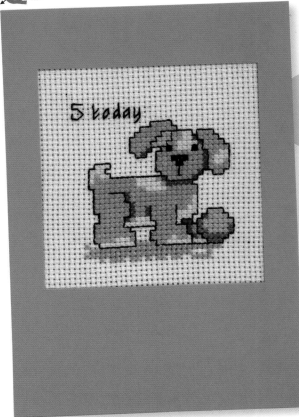

Finished design size on 14-count
5.6 x 5.8cm (2¼ x 2⅜in)

Cute Puppy

This sweet puppy will bring a smile. Change the birthday number using the chart on page 102.

You Will Need
- 15cm x 15cm (6 x 6in) 14-count white Aida
- Double-fold card to fit embroidery

Stitch and make up your card –
see Quick Stitch, page 5.

Quicker

Finished design size on 14-count
4.5 x 5.6cm (1¾ x 2¼in)

Tug Boat Fun

This bright card is sure to be popular with young boys. Change the birthday number using the chart on page 102.

You Will Need
- 13 x 15cm (5 x 6in)
14-count white Aida
- Double-fold card to fit embroidery

Stitch and make up your card –
see Quick Stitch, page 5.

Quickest

Football Forever

This is a great gift tag for a budding footballer. Change the number using the chart on page 102.

Finished design size on 14-count
1.8 x 1.8cm (¾ x ¾in)

You Will Need
- 10 x 10cm (4 x 4in) 14-count dark green Aida
- Red card for tag 11.4 x 9cm (4½ x 3½in)
- Iron-on interfacing • Ribbon to trim

Follow Quick Stitch, page 5. Make a decorative-edged card (page 98) and punch a hole in the top left corner. Back the embroidery with iron-on interfacing (page 97), trim to 4cm (1½in) square and mount on the tag. Tie on the ribbon bow.

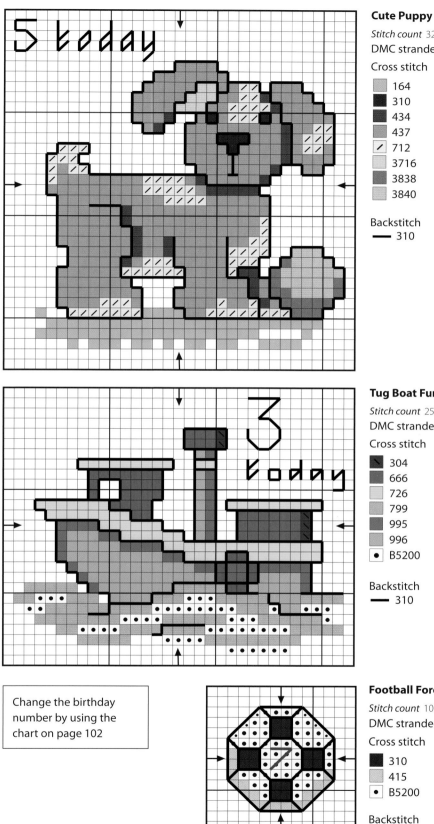

Cute Puppy

Stitch count 32h x 31w

DMC stranded cotton

Cross stitch

	164
■	310
■	434
	437
╱	712
	3716
	3838
	3840

Backstitch
— 310

Tug Boat Fun

Stitch count 25h x 31w

DMC stranded cotton

Cross stitch

◣	304
	666
	726
	799
	995
	996
•	B5200

Backstitch
— 310

Change the birthday number by using the chart on page 102

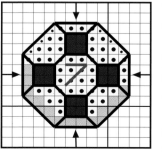

Football Forever

Stitch count 10h x 10w

DMC stranded cotton

Cross stitch

■	310
	415
•	B5200

Backstitch
— 310
— 666

Designs by Claire Crompton

Finished design size on 14-count 9.3 x 7.8cm (3¾ x 3in)

Quick

Official Grown-up!

Being 18 makes you a grown-up – doesn't it? Make the card for a 21st birthday by working '21' in the balloon instead of '18'.

You Will Need
- 19.5 x 18cm (7¾ x 7in) 14-count white Aida
- Double-fold card to fit embroidery

Follow Quick Stitch, page 5 but using two strands for backstitch where indicated on the chart key.

Quicker

21 Today!

All the ingredients for a wonderful 21st birthday!

You Will Need
- 13 x 20.3cm (5 x 8in) 14-count white Aida
- Single-fold card to fit embroidery
- Heavyweight iron-on interfacing

Follow Quick Stitch, page 5, using two strands for backstitch. Iron two layers of interfacing, one at a time, on the back of the embroidery (page 97). Trim to within four blocks on all sides, cutting around the cork. Mount on the card.

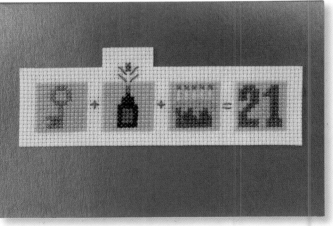

Finished design size on 14-count 3.3 x 11.6cm (1¼ x 4½in)

Quickest

Finished design size on 14-count
3 x 3cm (1¼ x 1¼in)

Big Number

18 or 21 is a big number in someone's life.

You Will Need
- 7.6 x 7.6cm (3 x 3in) 14-count white Aida
- Single-fold card to fit embroidery
- Stick-on sequins

Stitch and make up your card – see Quick Stitch, page 5. Trim the embroidery to within two blocks on all sides. Mount on the card and cover the edges with stick-on sequins.

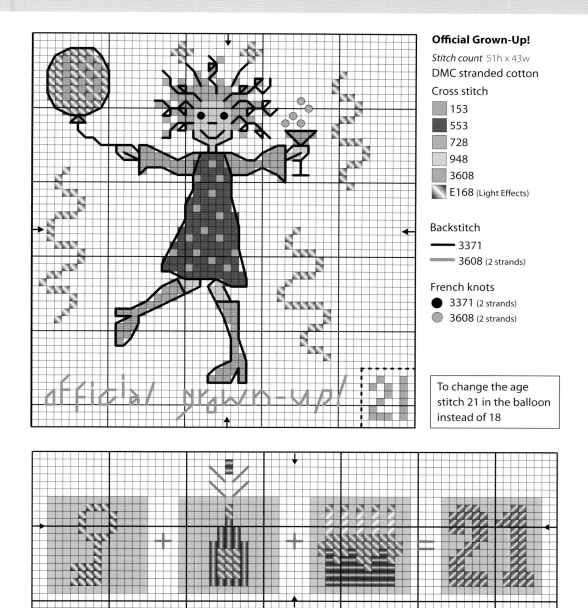

Official Grown-Up!

Stitch count 51h x 43w

DMC stranded cotton

Cross stitch

- 153
- 553
- 728
- 948
- 3608
- E168 (Light Effects)

Backstitch

- —— 3371
- —— 3608 (2 strands)

French knots

- ● 3371 (2 strands)
- ○ 3608 (2 strands)

To change the age stitch 21 in the balloon instead of 18

21 Today!

Stitch count 18h x 64w

DMC stranded cotton and Light Effects threads

Cross stitch

- E211
- E316
- E415
- E436
- E699
- 772
- E3852
- E5200

Backstitch

- —— E436 (2 strands)

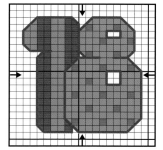 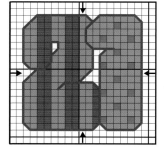

Big Number

Stitch count 17h x 17w

DMC stranded cotton

Cross stitch

- 208
- 602
- 704
- 959

Backstitch

- —— 803

Finished design size on 14-count 10 x 10cm (4 x 4in)

Grown Ups?

This is the perfect card for someone you know who's young at heart. Change the birthday number using the chart opposite.

You Will Need
- 20 x 20cm (8 x 8in) 14-count white Aida
- Double-fold card to fit embroidery

Stitch and make up your card – see Quick Stitch, page 5.

Naughty 40

Use metallic threads to make a fortieth birthday a glittering and fun milestone.

You Will Need
- 18 x 18cm (7 x 7in) 14-count white Aida
- Double-fold card to fit embroidery

Stitch and make up your card – see Quick Stitch, page 5.

Finished design size on 14-count 7.5 x 7.5cm (2⅞ x 2⅞in)

Birthday Cake

This birthday cake is just for one but made more special with a little ribbon bow. Change the birthday number using the chart opposite.

You Will Need
- 10 x 10cm (4 x 4in) 14-count white Aida
- Gift tag to fit embroidery • Thin pink ribbon

Follow Quick Stitch, page 5. Back the embroidery with interfacing (page 97). Thread the ribbon from the front of one side of the cake, to the back and out to the front on the other side. Tie in a bow. Trim and mount the embroidery on the tag.

Finished design size on 14-count 3.5 x 3.5cm (1⅜ x 1⅜in)

Grown-Ups?

Stitch count 54h x 54w

DMC stranded cotton

Cross stitch

- 744
- 907
- 917
- 920
- 948
- 3608
- 3846
- E211 (Light Effects)
- E3747 (Light Effects)

Backstitch

- —— 917 (2 strands)
- —— 3371

French knots

- ○ 744
- ● 3371

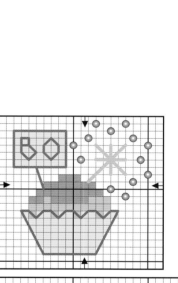

Birthday Cake

Stitch count 19h x 19w

DMC stranded cotton

Cross stitch

- 744
- 3609
- 3823

Backstitch

- —— 414

French knots

- ○ E168 (Light Effects)

Long stitch

- —— E168 (Light Effects)

Naughty 40

Stitch count 40h x 40w

DMC Light Effects thread

Cross stitch

- E155
- E703
- E3821
- E3849

Let's celebrate

There are many memorable events in our lives that deserve heartfelt congratulations – a wedding, the arrival of a baby, the celebration of an enduring marriage. Our lives are peppered with milestones; those wonderful 'hooray!' moments that deserve a hand-stitched card.

The following section has a wealth of great cross stitch designs, perfect for passing on our love, thoughts and best wishes. It may be that you want to congratulate someone on passing their driving test, or moving to a new home, or being promoted in their job or to wish them bon voyage as they embark on an exciting journey. The quick-to-stitch designs in this chapter mean that you'll be ready for them all.

To Have And To Hold Designs by Lesley Teare

Finished design size on 14-count 9.5 x 6cm (3¾ x 2⅜in)

Quick

Slice of Love

This lovely wedding cake design mounted in a gold foil card is sure to delight the happy couple.

You Will Need
- 15.5 x 13cm (6¼ x 5in) 14-count pale pink Aida
- Double-fold card to fit embroidery

Stitch and make up your card – see Quick Stitch, page 5.

Quicker

Finished design size on 14-count
9 x 6.8cm (3½ x 2¾in)

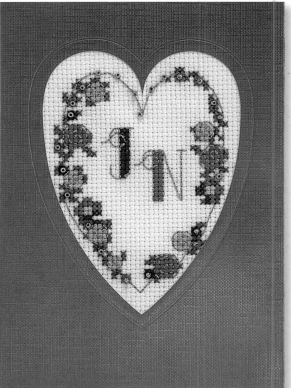

Hearts and Flowers

A card with a heart-shaped aperture enhances this pretty design. Use the alphabet charted on page 102 to change the initials.

Quickest

Lucky in Love

With this gift tag you can continue a wedding tradition of giving a wooden spoon for luck.

Finished design size
on 14-count
3.8 x 3cm (1½ x 1⅛in)

You Will Need
- 10 x 10cm (4 x 4in) 14-count white Aida
- Gold card for tag
- Iron-on interfacing
- Red ribbon for tie

Follow Quick Stitch, page 5. Make a tag from gold card (see page 98).

You Will Need
- 16.5 x 12cm (6½ x 4¾in) 14-count white Aida
- Double-fold card to fit embroidery (Impress Cards)
- Mill Hill seed beads 00557 gold

Stitch and make up your card – see Quick Stitch, page 5.

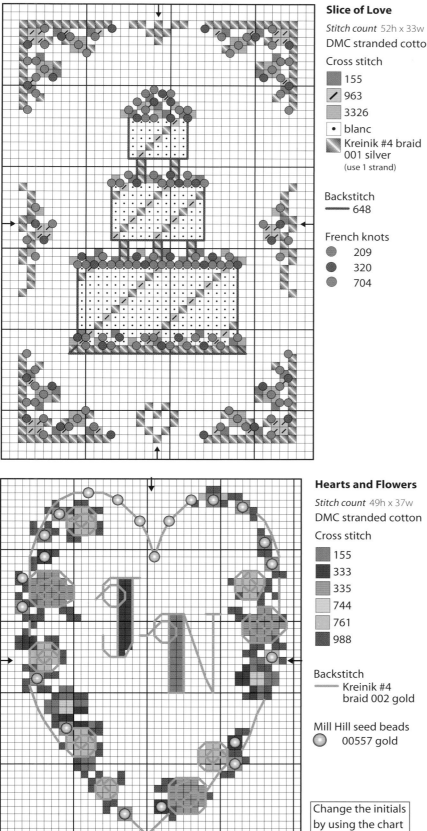

Slice of Love

Stitch count 52h x 33w
DMC stranded cotton

Cross stitch

▨	155
◪	963
▨	3326
•	blanc
▨	Kreinik #4 braid 001 silver (use 1 strand)

Backstitch
——— 648

French knots

●	209
●	320
●	704

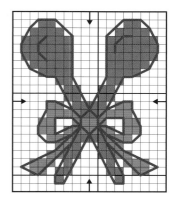

Hearts and Flowers

Stitch count 49h x 37w
DMC stranded cotton

Cross stitch

▨	155
▨	333
▨	335
▨	744
▨	761
▨	988

Backstitch
——— Kreinik #4 braid 002 gold

Mill Hill seed beads
○ 00557 gold

Change the initials by using the chart on page 102

Lucky in Love

Stitch count 20h x 16w
DMC stranded cotton

Cross stitch

▨	422
▨	760

Backstitch
——— 610

Finished design size on 18-count
9 x 9cm (3½ x 3½in)

Quick

Together in Love

Celebrate this joyful day of love and commitment with a card specially hand stitched for the happy couple.

You Will Need
- 24 x 24cm (9½ x 9½in) 18-count white Aida
- Double-fold card to fit embroidery
- Narrow gold ribbon to trim

Stitch and make up your card – see Quick Stitch, page 5.

Quicker

Finished design size on 14-count 6.7 x 6.7cm (2½ x 2½in)

Shared Dreams

A romantic sentiment and golden wedding rings make this card perfect for the occasion.

You Will Need
- 19 x 19cm (7½ x 7½in) 14-count white Aida
- Double-fold card to fit embroidery
- Narrow gold ribbon to trim

Stitch and make up your card – see Quick Stitch, page 5.

Quickest

Finished design size on 14-count
4.5 x 4.5cm (1¾ x 1¾in)

Wedding Bells

This simple motif with its gold border makes a lovely gift tag or small wedding card.

You Will Need
- 17.8 x 17.8cm (7 x 7in) 14-count white Aida
- Double-fold card/tag to fit embroidery
- Narrow white ribbon to trim

Stitch and make up your tag – see Quick Stitch, page 5.

Together in Love

Stitch count 65h x 65w

DMC stranded cotton

Cross stitch

■	469
■	470
✎	597
	598
▦	3687
⊙	3688
	3689
■	3810
•	blanc
◣	Kreinik #4 braid 028 citron (use 1 strand)

Backstitch

——	469
——	3810
——	Kreinik #4 braid 028 citron

French knots

◉	3687

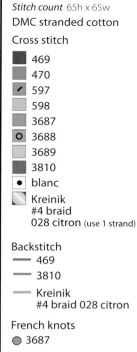

Shared Dreams

Stitch count 37h x 37w

DMC stranded cotton

Cross stitch

▨	470
✎	597
▦	3687
⊙	3688
	3689
◣	Kreinik #4 braid 028 citron (use 1 strand)

Backstitch

——	310
——	469
——	Kreinik #4 braid 028 citron

French knots

◉	3687
○	Kreinik #4 braid 028 citron

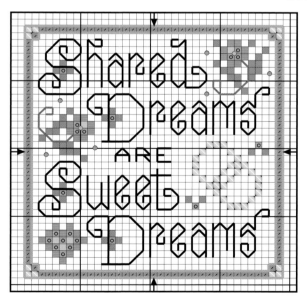

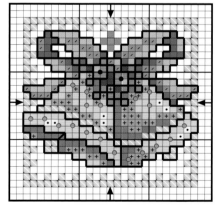

Wedding Bells

Stitch count 25h x 25w

DMC stranded cotton

Cross stitch

■	469		676
■	470	+	729
✎	597	▦	3687
	598		3689

■	3810
▨	3829
•	blanc
◣	Kreinik #4 braid 028 citron (use 1 strand)

Backstitch

——	310

French knots

●	310
◉	3687

Celebrate Silver Designs by Lesley Teare

Quick

Finished design size on 14-count 7.6 x 8cm (3 x 3¹⁄₈in)

Say it with Flowers

Celebrate a 25th wedding anniversary with this pretty card. Use the chart on page 102 to change the number.

You Will Need
- 14 x 14cm (5½ x 5½in) 14-count white Aida
- Double-fold card to fit embroidery

Stitch and make up your card –
see Quick Stitch, page 5.

Quicker

Two's Company

These doves signify peace and the joy in each other's company. To change the dates, see page 102.

You Will Need
- 18 x 12cm (7 x 4¾in) 14-count white Aida
- Double-fold card to fit embroidery

Stitch and make up your card –
see Quick Stitch, page 5.

Finished design size on 14-count 10 x 5.3cm (4 x 2in)

Quickest

Peace and Harmony

This peace dove is ideal as a tag on an anniversary gift. Change the number by using any of the large numbers charted on page 102.

*Finished design size on 14-count
3.3 x 3.5cm (1¼ x 1³⁄₈in)*

You Will Need
- 10 x 10cm (4 x 4in) 14-count Aida in white
- Mauve card for tag • Iron-on interfacing
- Narrow lilac ribbon

Follow Quick Stitch on page 5. Make a tag from mauve card (see page 98).

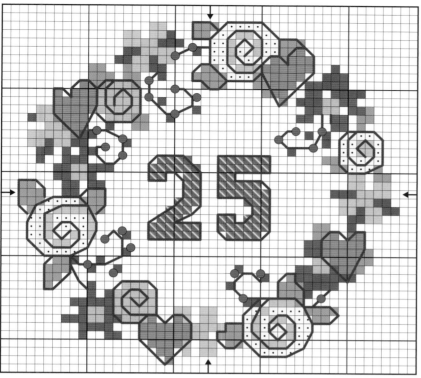

Say it with Flowers

Stitch count 41h x 44w

DMC stranded cotton

Cross stitch

■	208
■	562
■	563
■	963
■	3805
■	3855
•	B5200
▨	Kreinik #4 braid 001 silver (use 1 strand)

Backstitch
— 167

French knots
● 208

> Change the number by using the chart on page 102

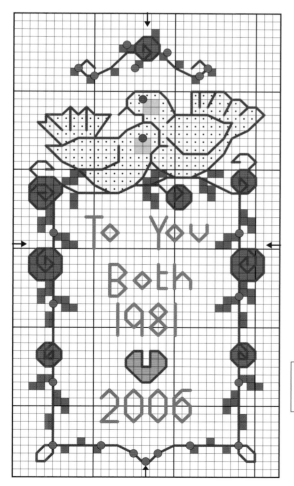

Two's Company

Stitch count 55h x 29w

DMC stranded cotton

Cross stitch

■	208
■	562
■	963
■	3833
•	B5200

Backstitch
— 167
— Kreinik #4 braid 001HL silver

French knots
● 167
● 208

> Change the dates by using the chart on page 102

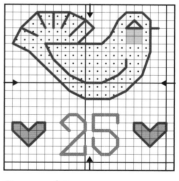

Peace and Harmony

Stitch count 18h x 19w

DMC stranded cotton

Cross stitch

■	963
■	3833
•	B5200

Backstitch
— 167
— Kreinik #4 braid 001 silver (use 1 strand)

Quick

Finished design size on 14-count 7.3 x 13.8cm (2¾ x 5½in)

Baby Girl

Stitch this pretty design to celebrate the birth of a baby girl. The motifs could also be stitched individually on small gifts such as booties or a bib.

You Will Need
- 18cm x 23cm (7 x 9in) 14-count white Aida
- Double-fold card to fit embroidery

Stitch and make up your card –
see Quick Stitch, page 5.

Quicker

Finished design size on 14-count 5.2 x 5.2cm (2 x 2in)

Pink Rabbit

This pretty little rabbit all in baby pinks is sure to be a favourite.

You Will Need
- 18 x 13cm (7 x 5in) 14-count ivory Aida
- Double-fold card to fit embroidery
- Ribbons to trim

Stitch and make up your card –
see Quick Stitch, page 5.

Quickest

Finished design size on 14-count
4.4 x 3.8cm (1¾ x 1½in)

She's Arrived!

This stork motif is also suitable for a gift bag. The frayed cord makes a pretty finishing touch.

You Will Need
- 10 x 10cm (4 x 4in) 14-count white Lurex Aida
- Double-fold card to fit embroidery • Cord to trim

Stitch and make up your card or tag – see Quick Stitch, page 5. Punch a hole in the top left corner of the card for the cord tassel embellishment.

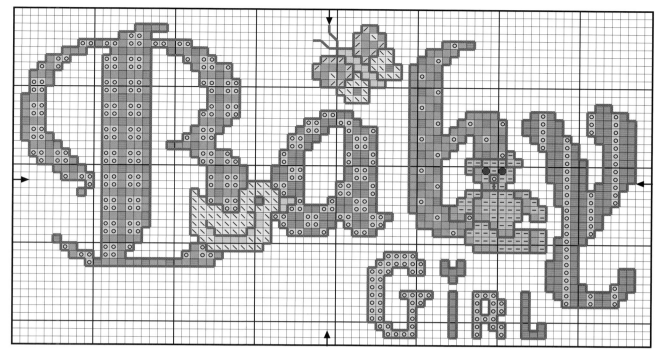

Baby Girl

Stitch count 40h x 76w

DMC stranded cotton

Cross stitch

210	437	− 739	\ 745	
✓ 211	603	744	○ 963	

Backstitch
— 414

French knots
● 414

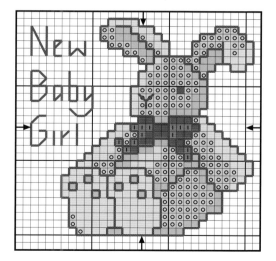

Pink Rabbit

Stitch count 29h x 29w

DMC stranded cotton

Cross stitch

150	○ 963
317	3716
819	ı 3731

Backstitch
— 317

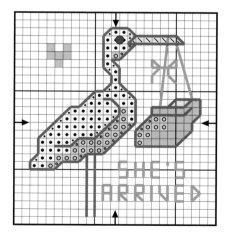

She's Arrived!

Stitch count 24h x 21w

DMC stranded cotton

Cross stitch
- \ 745
- 948
- ○ 963
- 3716
- • B5200

Backstitch
— 414
— 602

French knots
● 414

It's A Boy! Designs by Joanne Sanderson

Quick

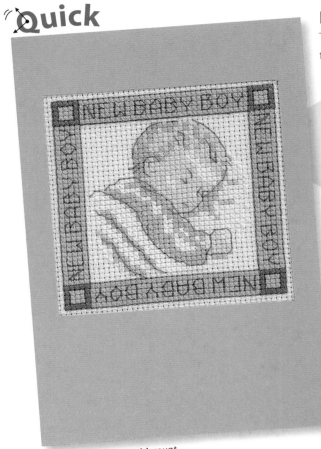

Baby Boy

This is the perfect card for that special occasion – the birth of an adorable baby boy.

You Will Need
- 18cm x 18cm (7 x 7in) 14-count antique white Aida
- Double-fold card to fit embroidery

Stitch and make up your card – see Quick Stitch, page 5.

Finished design size on 14-count
7.8 x 7.8cm (3 x 3in)

Moon Teddy

A sweet design to celebrate the arrival of a baby boy. For a girl, change the backstitch and bow to pink. The word 'girl' is charted on page 102.

Quicker

You Will Need
- 13 x 18cm (5 x 7in) 14-count white Aida
- Double-fold card to fit embroidery
- Ribbon bow to trim

Stitch and make up your card – see Quick Stitch, page 5. Stick the bow to the card.

Finished design size on 14-count
5.2 x 5.2cm (2 x 2in)

Toy Duck

This cute little motif can be also stitched on to a bib or booties as a gift.

Quickest

You Will Need
- 10 x 10cm (4 x 4in) 14-count white Aida
- Green card for tag 11.5 x 9cm (4½ x 3½in)
- Iron-on interfacing • Ribbon to trim

Follow Quick Stitch, page 5. Make a tag (page 98). Back the embroidery with iron-on interfacing (page 97) and mount on the tag. Trim with ribbon.

Finished design size on 14-count
2.9 x 2.9cm (1⅛ x 1⅛in)

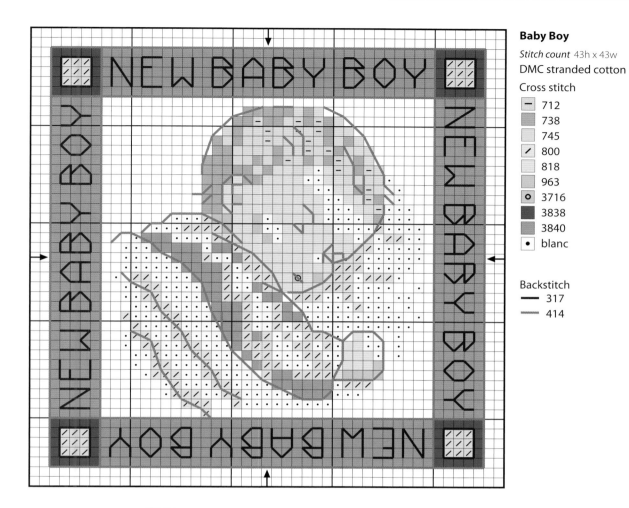

Baby Boy

Stitch count 43h x 43w

DMC stranded cotton

Cross stitch

−	712
	738
	745
╱	800
	818
	963
○	3716
	3838
	3840
•	blanc

Backstitch

— 317
— 414

Moon Teddy

Stitch count 29h x 29w

DMC stranded cotton

Cross stitch

	317
	437
╲	726
I	739
	744
	798
	827
•	blanc

Backstitch

— 317
— 798 long stitch

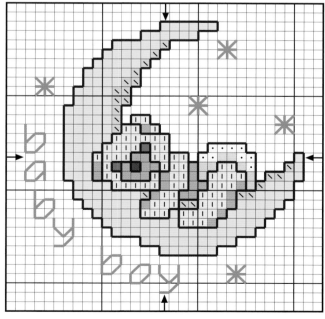

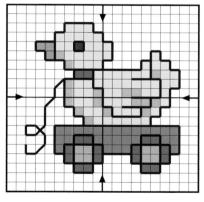

Toy Duck

Stitch count 16h x 16w

DMC stranded cotton

Cross stitch

		Backstitch
	317	— 317
	702	
	740	
	743	
	744	
	3839	

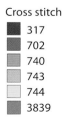

Blessed New Arrival Designs by Joan Elliott

Quick

Gift of Love

Babies are a precious gift and you can wish a sweet welcome to the new arrival with this adorable card.

You Will Need

- 24 x 24cm (9½ x 9½in) 18-count antique white Aida
- Double-fold card to fit embroidery
- Decorative ribbon to trim

Stitch and make up your card – see Quick Stitch, page 5.

Finished design size on 18-count 9 x 9cm (3½ x 3½in)

Quicker

A New Arrival

Welcome the new bundle of joy with this fun card design. A decorative ribbon adds a special touch.

You Will Need

- 19 x 19cm (7½ x 7½in) 14-count antique white Aida
- Double-fold card to fit embroidery
- Decorative ribbon to trim

Stitch and make up your card – see Quick Stitch, page 5.

Finished design size on 14-count 6.7 x 6.7cm (2½ x 2½in)

Quickest

Sssh, Baby Sleeping

This charming motif is very quick to stitch but perfect for the occasion.

You Will Need

- 17.8 x 17.8cm (7 x 7in) 14-count antique white Aida
- Double-fold card/tag to fit embroidery
- Narrow yellow ribbon to trim

Stitch and make up your tag – see Quick Stitch, page 5.

Finished design size on 14-count
4.5 x 4.5cm (1¾ x 1¾in)

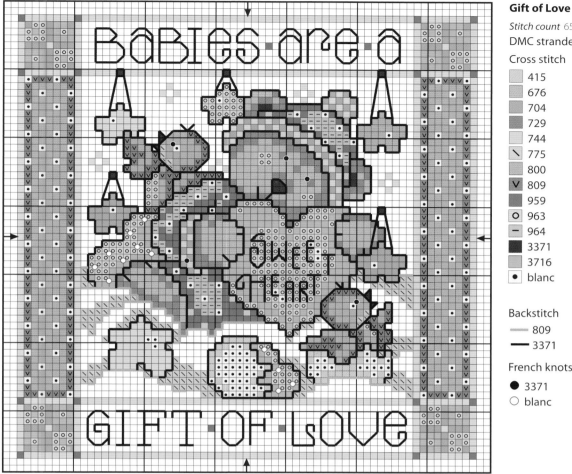

Gift of Love

Stitch count 65h x 65w

DMC stranded cotton

Cross stitch

	415
	676
	704
	729
	744
\	775
	800
V	809
	959
O	963
−	964
	3371
	3716
•	blanc

Backstitch

▬▬	809
▬▬	3371

French knots

●	3371
○	blanc

New Arrival

Stitch count 37h x 37w

DMC stranded cotton

Cross stitch

	704
	744
\	775
	800
V	809
	948
	959
O	963
−	964
	3716

Backstitch

▬▬	3371

French knots

●	3371
○	blanc

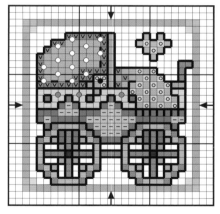

Sssh, Baby Sleeping

Stitch count 25h x 25w

DMC stranded cotton

Cross stitch

	676		959
	704	O	963
	729	−	964
	744		3371
	800		3716
V	809		

Backstitch

▬▬	3371

French knots

●	809
●	3371
○	blanc

Designs by Joanne Sanderson

Quick

Twin Bundles of Joy

This lovely card with its cute elephants can be stitched for the birth of twin girls or boys as the sunny yellows are unisex.

You Will Need

- 18 x 23cm (7 x 9in) 14-count white Aida

- Double-fold card to fit embroidery

Stitch and make up your card – see Quick Stitch, page 5.

Finished design size on 14-count 5.4 x 11cm (2⅛ x 4¼in)

Quicker

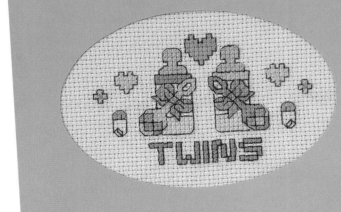

Finished design size on 14-count 5.4 x 9cm (2⅛ x 3½in)

It's Twins!

This card celebrates a twin birth, in this case a boy and a girl, but the motif colours can easily be changed.

You Will Need

- 13 x 18cm (5 x 7in) 14-count white Aida

- Double-fold card to fit embroidery

Stitch and make up your card – see Quick Stitch, page 5.

Quickest

Two to Love

This simple gift tag design could be stitched in any colour, perhaps to use up leftover threads.

You Will Need

- 10 x 10cm (4 x 4in) 14-count white Aida

- Blue card for tag 11.5 x 9cm (4½ x 3½in)

- Iron-on interfacing • Ribbon to trim

Follow Quick Stitch, page 5. Make a tag (page 98). Back the embroidery with iron-on interfacing (page 97) and stick on the tag. Tie the ribbon on in a bow.

Finished design size on 14-count 4 x 3cm (1½ x 1⅛in)

Twin Bundles of Joy

Stitch count 30h x 60w

DMC stranded cotton

Cross stitch

■	604	＼	746
■	743	▨	964
○	744	■	3812
▨	745		

Backstitch
—— 317

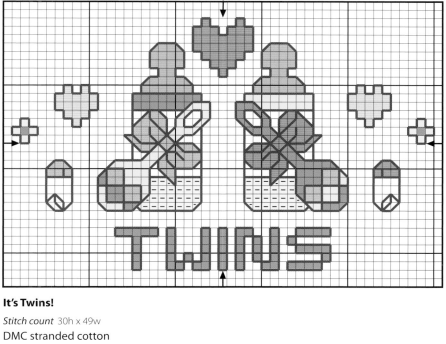

It's Twins!

Stitch count 30h x 49w

DMC stranded cotton

Cross stitch

■	353	−	712	■	954	▨	3840
■	604	▨	727	▨	963		

Backstitch
—— 317

Two to Love

Stitch count 22h x 16w

DMC stranded cotton

Cross stitch

■	156
■	743
▨	963

Backstitch
—— 333

Good Luck To You   Designs by Joan Elliott

Finished design size on 18-count
9 x 9cm (3½ x 3½in)

Quick

May Your Heart Be Light
Wish a special someone good luck with these words of support and singing bluebirds.

You Will Need
- 24 x 24cm (9½ x 9½in) 18-count white Aida
- Double-fold card to fit embroidery
- Narrow ribbon to trim

Stitch and make up your card – see Quick Stitch, page 5.

Quicker

Finished design size on 14-count
6.7 x 6.7cm (2½ x 2½in)

Follow Your Dreams
This happy teddy wishes someone special in your life good luck as they embark on a new venture.

You Will Need
- 19 x 19cm (7½ x 7½in) 14-count white Aida
- Double-fold card to fit embroidery
- Narrow ribbon to trim

Stitch and make up your card – see Quick Stitch, page 5.

Quickest

Finished design size on 14-count
4.5 x 4.5cm (1¾ x 1¾in)

Good Luck
A golden horseshoe and a four-leaf clover – what more luck could you need?

You Will Need
- 17.8 x 17.8cm (7 x 7in) 14-count white Aida
- Double-fold card/tag to fit embroidery
- Narrow ribbon to trim

Stitch and make up your tag – see Quick Stitch, page 5.

May Your Heart Be Light

Stitch count 65h x 65w

DMC stranded cotton

Cross stitch

- 310
- 312
- / 334
- 351
- 352
- 420
- 422
- 598
- 906
- 907
- 3755
- 3821
- O 3852
- • blanc

Backstitch
— 310

French knots
- ● 310
- ◉ 351

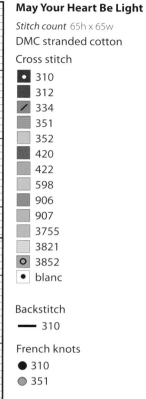

Follow Your Dreams

Stitch count 37h x 37w

DMC stranded cotton

Cross stitch

- 310
- 312
- 351
- 352
- 420
- 422
- 906
- 907
- 3821
- \ 3822
- O 3852
- • blanc

Backstitch
— 310

French knots
- ● 310

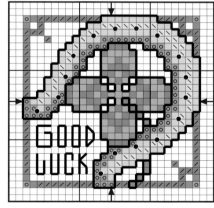

Good Luck

Stitch count 25h x 25w

DMC stranded cotton

Cross stitch | | Backstitch
- / 334 | 3821 | — 310
- 906 | \ 3822 |
- 907 | O 3852 |

French knots
- ● 310

Quick

New Horizons

Send this card to someone on the move, whether to a new job, a new town or even a new country.

You Will Need

- 15 x 12.5cm (6 x 5in) 14-count pale lemon Aida
- Double-fold card with arched aperture to fit embroidery (Impress Cards)

Stitch and make up your card – see Quick Stitch, page 5.

Finished design size on 14-count 7.5 x 5cm (3 x 2in)

Quicker

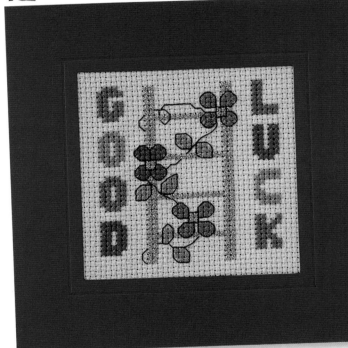

Finished design size on 14-count 6.3 x 6.3cm (2½ x 2½in)

Ladder of Success

This ladder of success is stitched in gold metallic thread – perfect to congratulate someone on their new job.

You Will Need

- 15 x 15cm (6 x 6in) 14-count pale green Aida
- Double-fold card to fit embroidery

Stitch and make up your card – see Quick Stitch, page 5.

Quickest

Pot of Gold

A gift given to celebrate a promotion at work will be valued even more with this little tag attached.

You Will Need

- 10 x 10cm (4 x 4in) 14-count pale green Aida
- Green card for tag • Iron-on interfacing • Gold cord for tie

Follow Quick Stitch, page 5.
Make the tag (see page 98).

Finished design size on 14-count
2.7 x 3cm (1 x 1¼in)

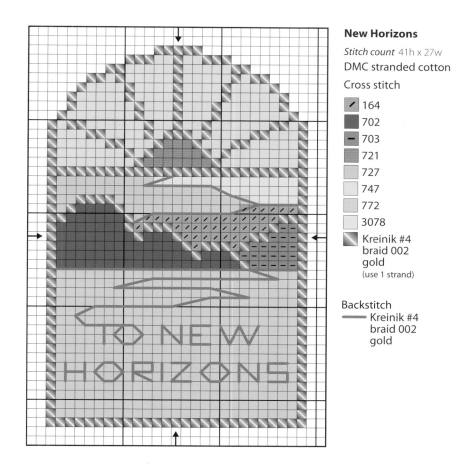

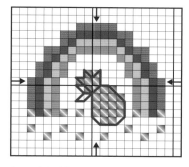

New Horizons

Stitch count 41h x 27w

DMC stranded cotton

Cross stitch

✓	164
■	702
−	703
▨	721
▨	727
▨	747
▨	772
▨	3078
◩	Kreinik #4 braid 002 gold (use 1 strand)

Backstitch

— Kreinik #4 braid 002 gold

Pot of Gold

Stitch count 15h x 17w

DMC stranded cotton

Cross stitch

▨	351	▨	553
■	701	◩	Kreinik #4 braid 002 gold (use 1 strand)
▨	742		

Backstitch

— 869

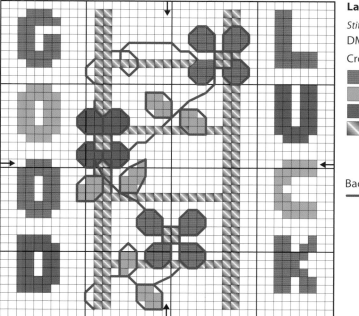

Ladder of Success

Stitch count 35h x 35w

DMC stranded cotton

Cross stitch

▨	553
▨	704
■	798
◩	Kreinik #4 braid 002 gold (use 1 strand)

Backstitch

— 561

Welcome To Your New Home Designs by Joan Elliott

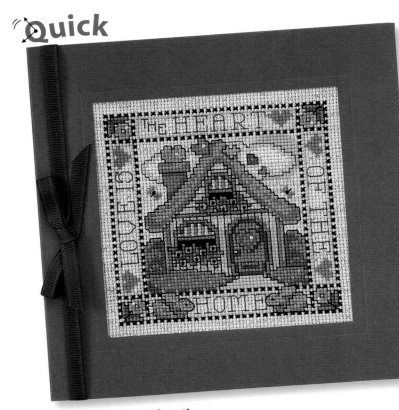

Finished design size on 18-count
9 x 9cm (3½ x 3½in)

Heart of the Home

Congratulate new home owners with this delightfully colourful card celebrating the comforts of love and home.

You Will Need
- 24 x 24cm (9½ x 9½in) 18-count Fiddler's Light Aida
- Double-fold card to fit embroidery
- Narrow ribbon to trim

Stitch and make up your card – see Quick Stitch, page 5.

Quicker

Home Sweet Home

This traditional phrase still says it all.

You Will Need
- 19 x 19cm (7½ x 7½in) 14-count Fiddler's Light Aida
- Double-fold card to fit embroidery
- Narrow ribbon to trim

Stitch and make up your card – see Quick Stitch, page 5.

Finished design size on 14-count
6.7 x 6.7cm (2½ x 2½in)

Quickest

Finished design size on 14-count
4.5 x 4.5cm (1¾ x 1¾in)

Key to the Door

Stitch this design and mount in a sunny yellow card or tag to celebrate moving to a new home.

You Will Need
- 17.8 x 17.8cm (7 x 7in) 14-count Fiddler's Light Aida
- Double-fold card/tag to fit embroidery

Stitch and make up your tag – see Quick Stitch, page 5.

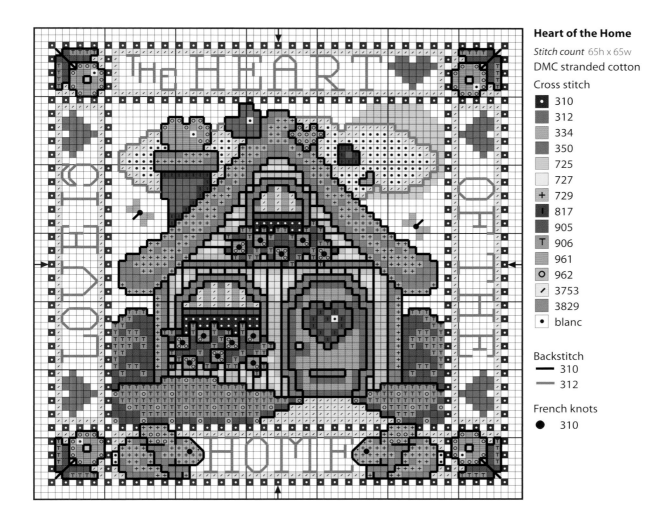

Heart of the Home

Stitch count 65h x 65w

DMC stranded cotton

Cross stitch

▣	310
▦	312
▨	334
▩	350
▨	725
☐	727
+	729
▌	817
▦	905
T	906
▨	961
O	962
╱	3753
▨	3829
•	blanc

Backstitch

— 310

— 312

French knots

● 310

Home Sweet Home

Stitch count 37h x 37w

DMC stranded cotton

Cross stitch

▦	312
▩	350
▨	725
T	906
▨	961
O	962
▨	3829

Backstitch

— 905

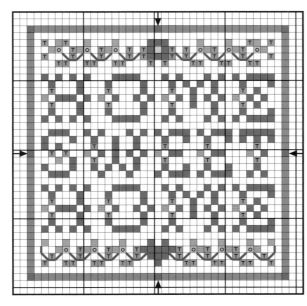

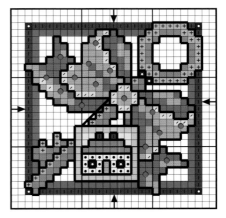

Key to the Door

Stitch count 25h x 25w

DMC stranded cotton

Cross stitch

▣ 310		▨ 725		╱ 3753	
▦ 312		☐ 727		▨ 3829	
▨ 334		+ 729		• blanc	
▩ 350		▌ 817			

Backstitch

— 310

French knots

● 350

Quick

Finished design size on 14-count
9.5 x 14.2cm (3¾ x 5½in)

Graduation

The sky's the limit for a new graduate so celebrate with this bright balloon and its message 'Genius for Hire'.

You Will Need
- 18 x 23cm (7 x 9in) 14-count light blue Aida
- Double-fold card to fit embroidery
- Tracing paper

Stitch and make up your card – see Quick Stitch, page 5. Shape the card aperture at the top of the balloon by drawing the shape on tracing paper. Transfer the shape to the card and cut it out. Mount the embroidery into the card.

Quicker

Super Star

Perfect for a sparkly superstar who's passed an exam, got a promotion, or graduated.

You Will Need
- 13 x 13cm (5 x 5in) 14-count white Aida
- Single-fold card to fit embroidery

Stitch and make up your card – see Quick Stitch, page 5. Trim the embroidery to about 7.5 x 7.5cm (3 x 3in) and then mount on to the card.

Finished design size on 14-count   7 x 5.7cm (2¾ x 2¼in)

Quickest

Finished design size on 14-count
4.2 x 3.3cm (1¾ x 1¼in)

Top Swot

Perfect for academic or music exams: let the world know that it's cool to be a swot with either a gift tag or a badge.

You Will Need
- 10 x 7.6cm (4 x 3in) 14-count white Aida
- Single-fold card to fit embroidery

Follow Quick Stitch, page 5. To make up as a gift tag, see page 98. To make up as a badge, see page 99.

Graduation

Stitch count 52h x 78w

DMC stranded cotton

Cross stitch

• blanc		434		644	/ 801			3866
414	O	498		666	I 814			

Backstitch

—— 801

—— 414 (2 strands)

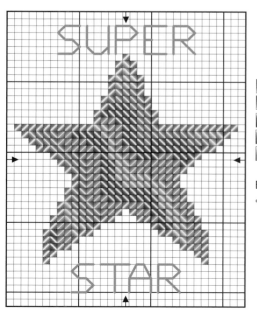

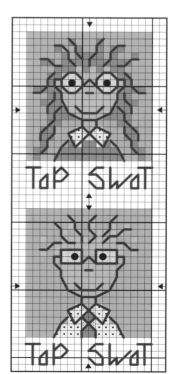

Super Star

Stitch count 38h x 31w

DMC Light Effects thread

Cross stitch

E168

E703

E718

E3849

E3852

Backstitch

—— E3849

(2 strands)

Top Swot

Stitch count 23h x 18w each

DMC stranded cotton

Cross stitch

• blanc

725

754

948

955

957

996

Backstitch

—— 3857

French knots

● 3857

Bon Voyage! Designs by Lesley Teare

Finished design size on 14-count
7.3 x 7.3cm (2⅞ x 2⅞in)

Quick

On the Way!
Stitch this cheerful design for a simple bon voyage card.

You Will Need
- 14 x 14cm (5½ x 5½in) 14-count pale blue Aida
- Double-fold card to fit embroidery

Stitch and make up your card – see Quick Stitch, page 5.

Quicker

Finished design size on 14-count
6.7 x 6.2cm (2¾ x 2½in)

His 'n' Hers
Send good wishes for a fabulous holiday with this eye-catching design in contrasting colours.

You Will Need
- 15 x 15cm (6 x 6in) 14-count pale lime Aida
- Double-fold card to fit embroidery • Red or pink felt-tip pen

Stitch and make up your card – see Quick Stitch, page 5. Use two strands for the long stitch in the bag handles. Decorate the card by drawing a line around the aperture using a red or pink pen.

Quickest

Snail's Progress
Stitch this fun design for a tag on a going-away gift.

You Will Need
- 10 x 10cm (4 x 4in) 14-count pale lime Aida
- Orange card for tag • Iron-on interfacing
- Lemon ribbon for tie

Follow Quick Stitch, page 5 and make a tag (page 98).

Finished design size on 14-count
2.5 x 1.8cm (1 x ¾in)

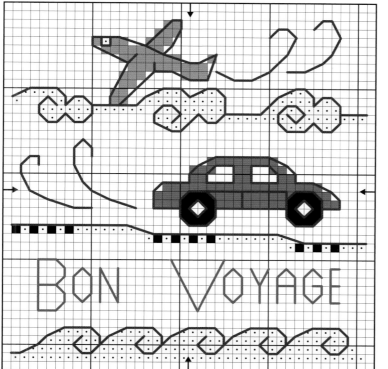

On the Way!

Stitch count 40h x 40w

DMC stranded cotton

Cross stitch

■ 310
■ 3607
■ 3819
• B5200

Backstitch
—— 869
—— 3350

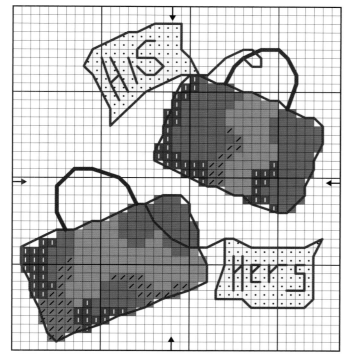

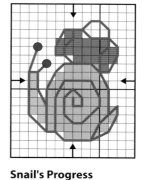

Snail's Progress

Stitch count 14h x 10w

DMC stranded cotton

Cross stitch
☐ 743
☐ 761
■ 922

Backstitch
—— 552

French knots
● 552

His 'n' Hers

Stitch count 37h x 34w

DMC stranded cotton

Cross stitch

| ╱ 166 | ■ 3607 | • B5200 |
| ▮ 718 | ■ 3819 | |

Backstitch
—— 869
(1 strand)

Long stitch
—— 869
(2 strands)

Designs by Claire Crompton

Quick

Finished design size on 14-count 7 x 12.5cm (2¾ x 5in)

Fab 'n' Funky

What every teenage driver desires:
a fab, funky car and freedom!

You Will Need

- 18 x 23cm (7 x 9in) 14-count white Aida
- Single-fold card to fit embroidery
- Heavyweight iron-on interfacing

Stitch and make up your card – see Quick Stitch, page 5. For tweeded threads, use one strand of each colour in the needle. Back the embroidery with two layers of iron-on interfacing, one at a time (page 97). Trim and cut the motifs apart or leave as a patch. Mount on the card.

Quicker

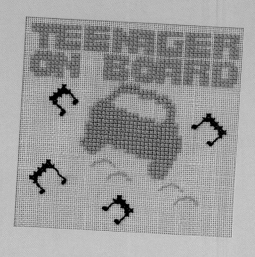

Finished design size on 28-count 9 x 9.3cm (3½ x 3⅝in)

Teenager on Board

Never mind 'baby on board', watch out other road users – there's a teenager about!

You Will Need

- 18 x 18cm (7 x 7in) 28-count light green evenweave
- Double-fold card to fit embroidery
- Heavyweight iron-on interfacing

Stitch and make up your card – see Quick Stitch, page 5 but use two strands for backstitch.

Quickest

Finished design size on 14-count
3.8 x 3.8cm (1½ x 1½in)

Safe Driving

A fluorescent smiley face makes an unusual gift tag or novelty hanging for the car.

You Will Need

- 9 x 9cm (3½ x 3½in) 14-count white Aida
- Gift tag to fit embroidery • Heavyweight iron-on interfacing

Follow Quick Stitch, page 5. Iron on two layers of interfacing, as for the card above. Trim, leaving three blocks all round. Thread a loop of red thread through the top. Pierce two holes in the card, thread the loop through and tie at the back.

Fab 'n' Funky

Stitch count 38h x 67w

DMC stranded cotton

Cross stitch

	165
	413
	553
	602
	608
	704
	718
	3325
	E168 (Light Effects)
	772 + E966 (Light Effects) (use 1 strand of each colour together in the needle)

Backstitch
—— 3371

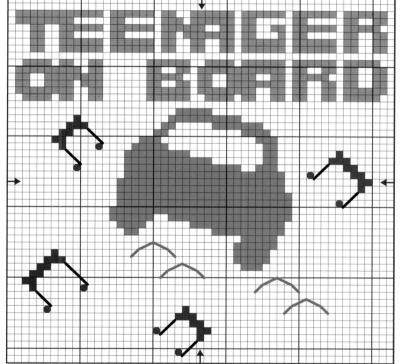

Teenager on Board

Stitch count 49h x 51w

DMC stranded cotton

Cross stitch

	310
	947
	3849

Backstitch
—— 310 (2 strands)
—— 3849 (2 strands)

French knots
● 310

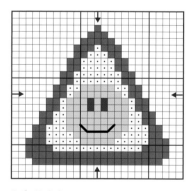

Safe Driving

Stitch count 21h x 21w

DMC stranded cotton

Cross stitch | Backstitch

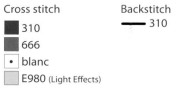

	310	—— 310
	666	
•	blanc	
	E980 (Light Effects)	

Days to remember

There are some days that come just once a year but have become a traditional, treasured celebration that we plan for, share with others and enjoy; and what better way than sending a cross stitch card?

There's Easter and Christmas of course and also romantic St Valentine's Day and spooky Hallowe'en. The important American celebrations of the Fourth of July and Thanksgiving are also ideal for card and gift giving.

So if you want to send a valentine to a loved one or to tell your mum or dad how very special they are, you will find plenty of choices in this final section, whether your taste is for the traditional, the quirky, the sentimental or the cute.

We
Three
Kings

Merry Christmas

Finished design size on 14-count 9.3 x 8.5cm (3¾ x 3⅜in)

Quick

You Make My Heart Sparkle

Show someone just how much they mean to you and your heart.

You Will Need
- 20.3 x 18cm (8 x 7in) 14-count white Aida
- Single-fold card to fit embroidery
- Heavyweight iron-on interfacing

Stitch and make up your card – see Quick Stitch, page 5. Iron on two layers of interfacing, one at a time (page 97). Trim to within five blocks on all sides, cutting around the curve of the text. Mount on the card.

Quicker

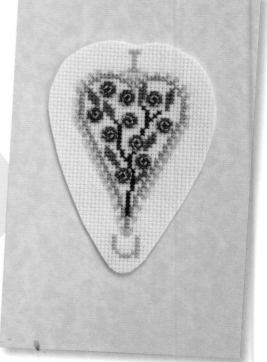

Finished design size on 14-count 10 x 5.2cm (4 x 2in)

I Love U

Give this heart as a token of your love.

You Will Need
- 18 x 13cm (7 x 5in) 14-count white Aida
- Mill Hill glass seed beads 02018 pink
- Single-fold card to fit embroidery

Stitch and make up your card – see Quick Stitch, page 5. Iron on interfacing (as above). On the back draw a heart shape around the stitching and cut around the shape. Mount on the card. Alternatively, use a ready-made card with a heart aperture.

Quickest

Finished design size on 14-count 5 x 3cm (2 x 1¼in)

Dotty About You

Bright, funky dots are sure to get your message across on Valentine's Day.

You Will Need
- 10 x 7.6cm (4 x 3in) 14-count white Aida
- Single-fold tag to fit embroidery
- Narrow ribbon for tie

Follow Quick Stitch, page 5. Trim and mount on the tag, punching a hole in the top left corner for the ribbon tie.

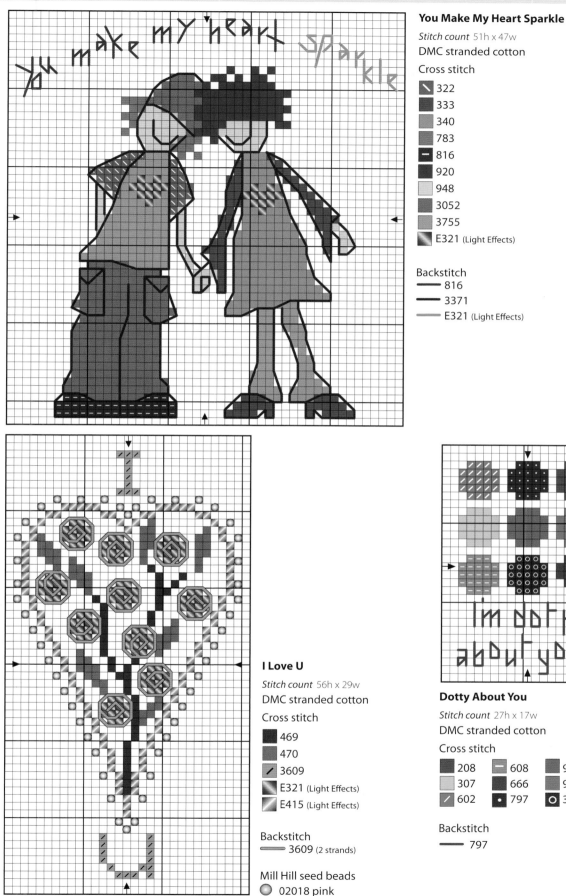

You Make My Heart Sparkle

Stitch count 51h x 47w

DMC stranded cotton

Cross stitch

◥	322
■	333
■	340
■	783
▬	816
■	920
☐	948
■	3052
■	3755
◪	E321 (Light Effects)

Backstitch

──	816
──	3371
──	E321 (Light Effects)

I Love U

Stitch count 56h x 29w

DMC stranded cotton

Cross stitch

■	469
■	470
◢	3609
◪	E321 (Light Effects)
◪	E415 (Light Effects)

Backstitch

──	3609 (2 strands)

Mill Hill seed beads

◯	02018 pink

Dotty About You

Stitch count 27h x 17w

DMC stranded cotton

Cross stitch

■ 208	▬ 608	■ 906
☐ 307	■ 666	■ 996
◢ 602	⊡ 797	◉ 3834

Backstitch

──	797

St Patrick's Day Designs by Joan Elliott

Quick

Finished design size on 18-count 9 x 9cm (3½ x 3½in)

Celtic Fairy Greeting

This Celtic greeting, which means 'Ireland forever', is perfect for celebrating the wearing of the green.

You Will Need
- 24 x 24cm (9½ x 9½in) 18-count Fiddler's Light Aida
- Double-fold card to fit embroidery
- Narrow ribbon to trim

Stitch and make up your card – see Quick Stitch, page 5.

Quicker

Happy St Patrick's Day

Pass on the luck of the Irish with this attractive card in emerald and gold.

You Will Need
- 19 x 19cm (7½ x 7½in) 14-count Fiddler's Light Aida
- Double-fold card to fit embroidery
- Narrow ribbon to trim

Stitch and make up your card – see Quick Stitch, page 5.

Finished design size on 14-count 6.7 x 6.7cm (2½ x 2½in)

Quickest

Finished design size on 14-count 4.5 x 4.5cm (1¾ x 1¾in)

Lucky Shamrock

Wish someone a happy St Patrick's Day with this lucky shamrock.

You Will Need
- 17.8 x 17.8cm (7 x 7in) 14-count Fiddler's Light Aida
- Double-fold card/tag to fit embroidery
- Narrow ribbon to trim

Stitch and make up your tag – see Quick Stitch, page 5.

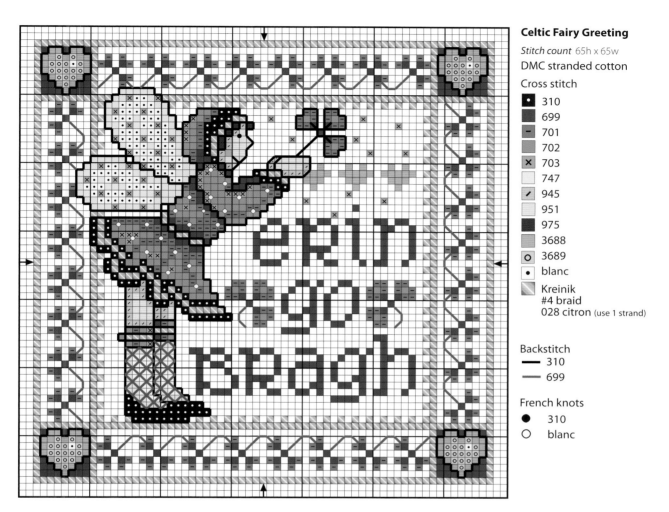

Celtic Fairy Greeting

Stitch count 65h x 65w

DMC stranded cotton

Cross stitch

- 310
- 699
- 701
- 702
- 703
- 747
- 945
- 951
- 975
- 3688
- 3689
- blanc
- Kreinik #4 braid 028 citron (use 1 strand)

Backstitch

- 310
- 699

French knots

- 310
- blanc

Happy St Patrick's Day

Stitch count 37h x 37w

DMC stranded cotton

Cross stitch

- 699
- 701
- 702
- 703
- 3688
- 3689
- 3829
- blanc

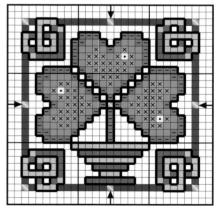

Lucky Shamrock

Stitch count 25h x 25w

DMC stranded cotton

Cross stitch

- 699
- 701
- 702
- 703
- 729
- 3829
- blanc
- Kreinik #4 braid 028 citron (use 1 strand)

Backstitch

- 310

Greetings At Easter Designs by Lesley Teare

Floral Cross

Stitch this pretty design full of multicoloured French knots for a traditional Easter card.

Quick

You Will Need

- 12.7 x 10cm (5 x 4in) 14-count lemon Aida
- Double-fold card with cross aperture to fit embroidery (Impress Cards)

Stitch and make up your card – see Quick Stitch, page 5.

Finished design size on 14-count 6.3 x 3.6cm (2½ x 1½in)

Easter Chick

This sweet little Easter chick surrounded by flowers makes a lovely Easter greeting.

Quicker

Finished design size on 14-count 5.2 x 5.5cm (2 x 2¼in)

You Will Need

- 12.5 x 12.5cm (5 x 5in) 14-count white Aida
- Double-fold card to fit embroidery

Stitch and make up your card – see Quick Stitch, page 5.

Daffodil Time

Quickest

A simple daffodil motif is a quick-stitch way to make a tag for an Easter gift or spring birthday card.

You Will Need

- 8 x 8cm (3 x 3in) 14-count pale yellow Aida
- Yellow card for tag • Iron-on interfacing
- Pale green ribbon for tie

Follow Quick Stitch, page 5, and then make a tag (see page 98).

Finished design size on 14-count 2.5 x 2.5cm (1 x 1in)

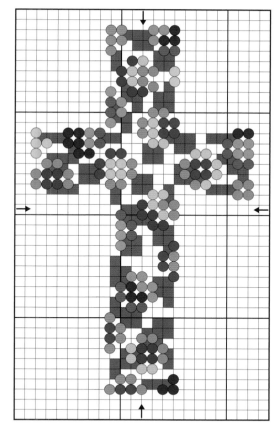

Floral Cross

Stitch count 35h x 20w

DMC stranded cotton

Cross stitch

■ 989

French knots
- ● 155
- ● 211
- ● 333
- ● 518
- ● 519
- ● 3607
- ● 3608
- ● 3689
- ● 3761

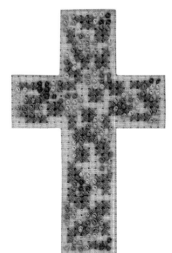

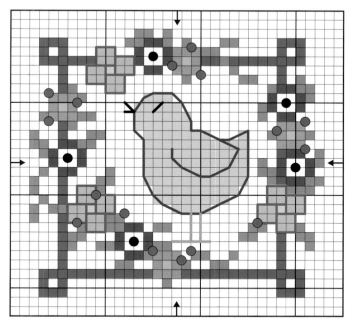

Easter Chick

Stitch count 29h x 31w

DMC stranded cotton

Cross stitch

■ 703	■ 798	■ 972
■ 761	■ 912	■ 3078

Backstitch
- ── 167
- ── 310
- ── 961
- ── 972

French knots
- ● 310
- ● 912

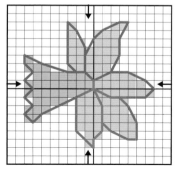

Daffodil Time

Stitch count 15h x 15w

DMC stranded cotton

Cross stitch
- ■ 744
- ■ 3078

Backstitch
- ── 721

Easter Fun   Designs by Joanne Sanderson

Quick

Easter Bunny with Gifts

Stitch this cute Easter bunny in a weekend for a fun Easter greeting.

You Will Need
- 20cm x 15cm (8 x 6in) 14-count white Aida
- Double-fold card to fit embroidery

Stitch and make up your card –
see Quick Stitch, page 5.

Finished design size on 14-count 10.7 x 6.7cm (4¼ x 2½in)

Cracking Fun

This cute chick is perfect for an Easter card. You could decorate the card with punched flower shapes in different colours.

Quicker

You Will Need
- 18 x 13cm (7 x 5in) 14-count white Aida
- Double-fold card to fit embroidery

Stitch and make up your card – see Quick Stitch, page 5.

Finished design size on 14-count
5.2 x 5.8cm (2 x 2¼in)

Quickest

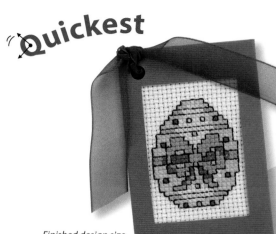

Easter Egg

This egg could be stitched in any colour, using up leftover threads.

You Will Need
- 10 x 10cm (4 x 4in) 14-count cream Aida
- Gift tag to fit embroidery • Ribbon to trim

Stitch and make up your card – see Quick Stitch, page 5.

*Finished design size
on 14-count*
4.4 x 3.4cm (1¾ x 1½in)

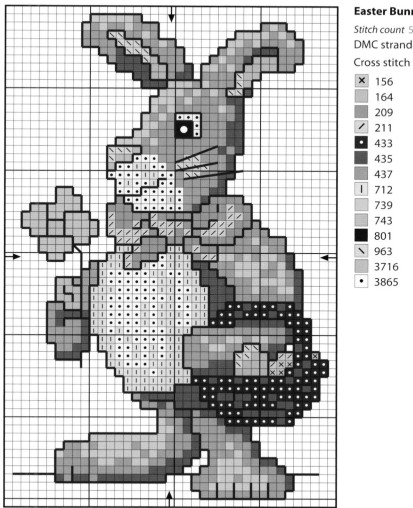

Easter Bunny with Gifts

Stitch count 59h x 37w

DMC stranded cotton

Cross stitch		Backstitch
☒	156	— 801
	164	
	209	**French knot**
◢	211	○ 3865 (eye)
⊡	433	
	435	
	437	
I	712	
	739	
	743	
■	801	
◥	963	
	3716	
•	3865	

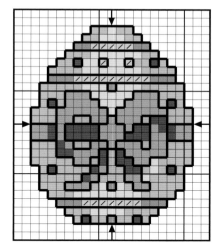

Easter Egg

Stitch count 24h x 19w

DMC stranded cotton

Cross stitch				Backstitch
	209		340	— 310
◢	211		743	
	333		745	

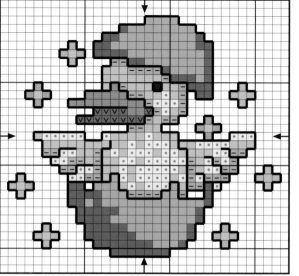

Cracking Fun

Stitch count 29h x 32w

DMC stranded cotton

Cross stitch

■	310
	603
	740
–	742
	743
•	746
	912
V	947
	955
	964
	3839

Backstitch

— 310

Quick

Finished design size on 14-count 6.5 x 12cm (2½ x 4¾in)

Mum's Garden

Mum's garden is a quirky place full of flowers in unusual pots.

You Will Need
- 15.2 x 23cm (6 x 9in) 14-count cream Aida
- Double-fold card to fit embroidery

Stitch and make up your card – see Quick Stitch, page 5.

A Perfect Mother's Day

A day for your lovely Mum to unwind with tea, cakes and a good book.

Quicker

You Will Need
- 15.2 x 20cm (6 x 8in) 14-count white Aida
- Double-fold card to fit embroidery
- Black felt-tip pen

Stitch and make up your card – see Quick Stitch, page 5. For tweeded cross stitches use one strand of each colour in the needle. Mount the stitching in the card and use a black pen to write your message.

Finished design size on 14-count 6 x 10cm (2⅜ x 4in)

Quickest

Finished design size on 14-count 4.5 x 3.8cm (1¾ x 1½in)

Best Mum

This design is great as a gift tag or why not make it into a badge so the world will know that you have the Best Mum!

You Will Need
- 9 x 9cm (3½ x 3½in) 14-count white Aida
- Single-fold card to fit embroidery

Follow Quick Stitch, page 5. To make up as a gift tag, see page 98. To make up as a badge, see page 99.

Mum's Garden

Stitch count 36h x 66w
DMC stranded cotton

Cross stitch

• blanc	543	⁄ 793	3347	I 3688	3836
157	792	3078	3687	3834	

Backstitch
— 839
— 3345 (2 strands)

French knots
157   3347
3345   3834

A Perfect Mother's Day

Stitch count 34h x 55w
DMC stranded cotton

Cross stitch

553	3371
⬊ 554	3609
744	3864
989	− 3865
3033	3747 + E3747 (Light Effects) (tweeded - use 1 strand of each colour in the needle)

Backstitch
— 3371

French knots
3609

Best Mum

Stitch count 25h x 21w
DMC stranded cotton

Cross stitch

210
602
725
754
E3852 (Light Effects)

Backstitch
— 3857

French knots
3857
E3852 (Light Effects)

Mums Are Special Designs by Lesley Teare

Finished design size on 14-count
8 x 5.8cm (3¼ x 2¼in)

Quick

Fanfare for Mum

This pretty floral design makes a lovely Mother's Day card set into an unusual fan-shaped aperture.

You Will Need
- 18 x 12.5cm (7 x 5in) 14-count white Aida
- Double-fold card with fan-shaped aperture to fit embroidery (Impress Cards)
- Pale pink ribbon bow

Stitch and make up your card – see Quick Stitch, page 5. Add a bow to finish.

Quicker

A Special Treat

A perfect card for a truly special mum.

You Will Need
- 12 x 12cm (5 x 5in) 14-count white Aida
- Double-fold card to fit embroidery
- Mill Hill seed beads 00557 gold

Stitch and make up your card –
see Quick Stitch, page 5.

Finished design size on 14-count 6.7 x 6.7cm (2⅝ x 2⅝in)

Quickest

For Mum

This pretty tag will make a Mother's Day gift even more memorable.

You Will Need
- 10 x 7.6cm (4 x 3in) 14-count white Aida
- Mauve card for tag • Iron-on interfacing
- Narrow lilac ribbon for tie

Stitch and make up your tag – see Quick Stitch, page 5. Make a tag (see page 98).

*Finished design size
on 14-count*
4.4 x 2.5cm (1¾ x 1in)

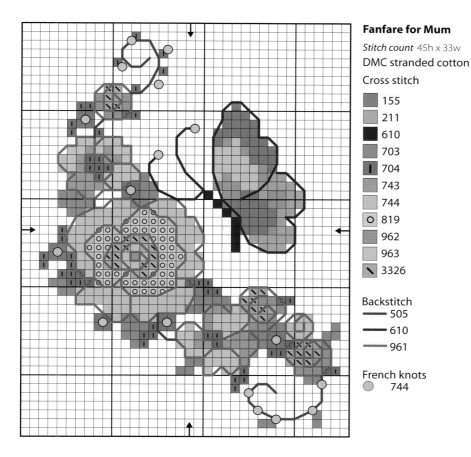

Fanfare for Mum

Stitch count 45h x 33w

DMC stranded cotton

Cross stitch

- 155
- 211
- 610
- 703
- | 704
- 743
- 744
- ○ 819
- 962
- 963
- \ 3326

Backstitch
— 505
— 610
— 961

French knots
○ 744

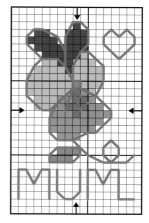

For Mum

Stitch count 24h x 15w

DMC stranded cotton

Cross stitch

- 333
- 703
- 721
- 744
- 972

Backstitch
— Kreinik #4 braid
002 gold

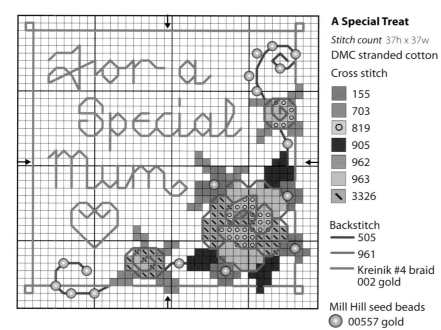

A Special Treat

Stitch count 37h x 37w

DMC stranded cotton

Cross stitch

- 155
- 703
- ○ 819
- 905
- 962
- 963
- \ 3326

Backstitch
— 505
— 961
— Kreinik #4 braid
002 gold

Mill Hill seed beads
○ 00557 gold

Dads Are Great Designs by Claire Crompton

Quick

Finished design size on 14-count 8.2 x 12cm (3¼ x 4¾in)

It's a Tie
Bright and colourful ties say so much about why you love your Dad!

You Will Need
- 18 x 22.5cm (7 x 9in) 14-count white Aida
- Double-fold card to fit embroidery

Stitch and make up your card – see Quick Stitch, page 5.

Quicker

It All Adds Up!
What does your dad need for a happy Father's Day? It's not hard to work it out!

You Will Need
- 12.5 x 20cm (5 x 8in) 14-count white Aida
- Single-fold card to fit embroidery

Stitch and make up your card – see Quick Stitch, page 5. For tweeded cross stitches, use one strand of each colour together in the needle.

Finished design size on 14-count 2.5 x 11cm (1 x 4½in)

Quickest

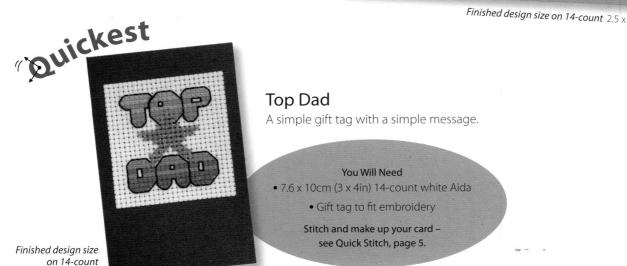

Top Dad
A simple gift tag with a simple message.

You Will Need
- 7.6 x 10cm (3 x 4in) 14-count white Aida
- Gift tag to fit embroidery

Stitch and make up your card – see Quick Stitch, page 5.

Finished design size on 14-count
3.8 x 3.5cm (1½ x 1⅜in)

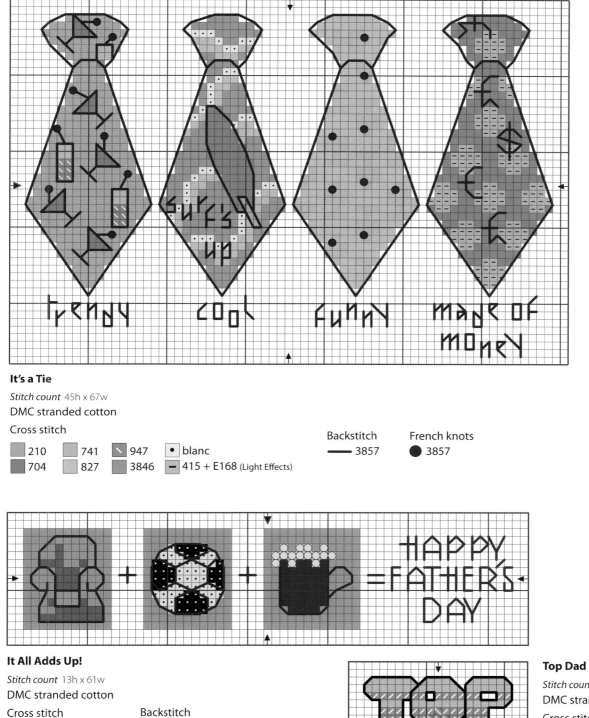

It's a Tie

Stitch count 45h x 67w

DMC stranded cotton

Cross stitch

| | 210 | | 741 | | 947 | • blanc |
| | 704 | | 827 | | 3846 | ▬ 415 + E168 (Light Effects) |

Backstitch
▬ 3857

French knots
● 3857

It All Adds Up!

Stitch count 13h x 61w

DMC stranded cotton

Cross stitch

	310
	780
	912
	954
•	blanc
	3325 + E334 (Light Effects) (tweeded - 1 strand of each colour in the needle)

Backstitch
▬ 823

French knots
○ blanc

Top Dad

Stitch count 21h x 19w

DMC stranded cotton

Cross stitch

	741
	900
	947
	E3852 (Light Effects)

Backstitch
▬ 310

Happy Father's Day   Designs by Lesley Teare

*Q*uick

Finished design size on 14-count 5 x 4.5cm (2 x 1¾in)

Dad's Chair

Stitch this cosy design for a dad who likes home comforts. You could use a felt-tip pen to write Happy Father's Day on the card front.

You Will Need
- 12.7 x 12.7cm (5 x 5in) 14-count pale blue Aida
- Double-fold card to fit embroidery

Stitch and make up your card – see Quick Stitch, page 5.

*Q*uicker

Finished design size on 14-count 6.8 x 4.2cm (2¾ x 1¾in)

Dad's Retreat

Show you dad how much you love him by stitching this charming scene.

You Will Need
- 18 x 16cm (7 x 6in) 14-count pale blue Aida
- Double-fold card with arched aperture to fit embroidery (Impress Cards)

Stitch and make up your card – see Quick Stitch, page 5.

*Q*uickest

Finished design size on 14-count 4.7 x 4.2cm (1⅞ x 1¾in)

Sport Mad

If your dad is a sports fanatic, this is the perfect tag for a Father's Day gift.

You Will Need
- 10 x 10cm (4 x 4in) 14-count white Aida
- Green card for tag • Iron-on interfacing
- Green ribbon for tie

Follow Quick Stitch, page 5.
Make a tag (see page 98).

Dad's Chair

Stitch count 27h x 25w
DMC stranded cotton

Cross stitch

- 164
- ▫ 310
- 349
- I 703
- 905
- 922
- 928
- · blanc

Backstitch
—— 898
—— 904

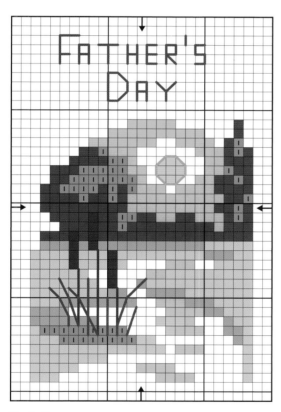

Dad's Retreat

Stitch count 37h x 23w
DMC stranded cotton

Cross stitch

		Backstitch
164	869	—— 743
I 703	905	—— 869
743	3825	—— 905
772		

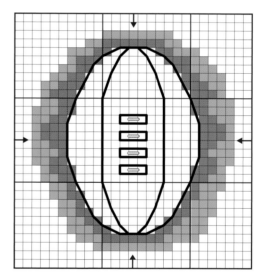

Sport Mad

Stitch count 26h x 23w
DMC stranded cotton

Cross stitch   Backstitch

- 704   —— 310
- 906   ═══ blanc

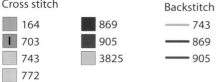

Celebrate Fourth Of July Designs by Joan Elliott

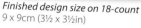

Quick

Let Freedom Ring

Bring out the red, white and blue for a birthday celebration of America's independence.

You Will Need
- 24 x 24cm (9½ x 9½in) 18-count Fiddler's Light Aida
- Double-fold card to fit embroidery
- Narrow ribbon to trim

Stitch and make up your card –
see Quick Stitch, page 5.

Finished design size on 18-count
9 x 9cm (3½ x 3½in)

Quicker

Have a Nice Day

This teddy could also be stitched for someone who's birthday is on the fourth of July.

You Will Need
- 19 x 19cm (7½ x 7½in) 14-count Fiddler's Light Aida
- Double-fold card to fit embroidery
- Narrow ribbon to trim

Stitch and make up your card –
see Quick Stitch, page 5.

Finished design size on 14-count 6.7 x 6.7cm (2½ x 2½in)

Quickest

Star Spangled

Gold metallic thread brings extra sparkle to this simple design.

You Will Need
- 17.8 x 17.8cm (7 x 7in) 14-count Fiddler's Light Aida
- Double-fold card/tag to fit embroidery
- Narrow ribbon for tie

Stitch and make up your tag –
see Quick Stitch, page 5.

Finished design size on 14-count
4.5 x 4.5cm (1¾ x 1¾in)

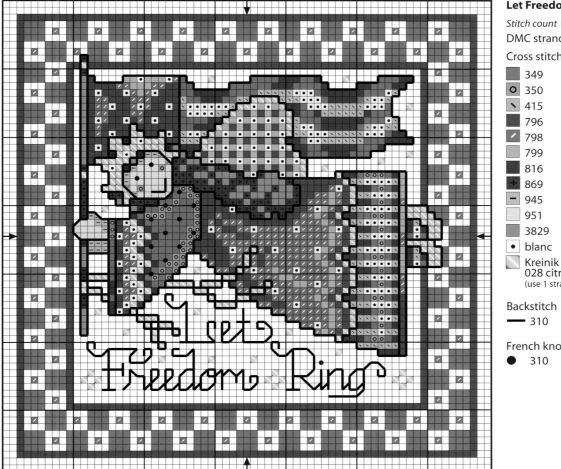

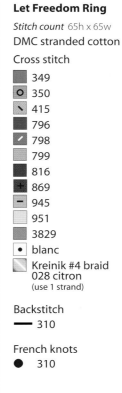

Let Freedom Ring

Stitch count 65h x 65w

DMC stranded cotton

Cross stitch

- 349
- ○ 350
- ╲ 415
- 796
- ╱ 798
- 799
- 816
- ＋ 869
- − 945
- 951
- 3829
- • blanc
- ╱ Kreinik #4 braid
  028 citron
  (use 1 strand)

Backstitch

— 310

French knots

● 310

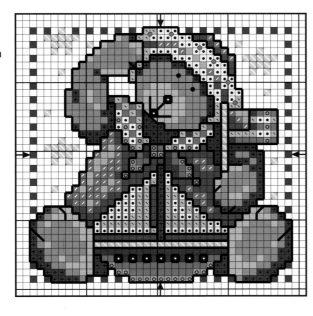

Have a Nice Day

Stitch count 37h x 37w

DMC stranded cotton

Cross stitch

- ⊡ 310
- 349
- ○ 350
- ╲ 415
- 729
- 796
- ╱ 798
- 799
- 816
- ＋ 869
- 3829
- • blanc
- ╱ Kreinik #4 braid
  028 citron
  (use 1 strand)

Backstitch

— 310
— 816

French knots

● 310
● 349

Star Spangled

Stitch count 25h x 25w

DMC stranded cotton

Cross stitch

349	╱ 798	╱ Kreinik
○ 350	816	#4 braid
╲ 415	• blanc	028 citron
796		(use 1 strand)

Backstitch

— 310
— Kreinik
  #4 braid
  028 citron

Happy Hallowe'en Designs by Joanne Sanderson

Quick

Finished design size on 14-count 6.2 x 6.1cm (2½ x 2½in)

Witching Hour

This witch looks like she's on her way to a great Hallowe'en party. Black fabric is used to represent the night sky.

You Will Need
- 13cm x 13cm (5 x 5in) 14-count black Aida
- Double-fold card to fit embroidery

Follow Quick Stitch, page 5 but use three strands for cross stitch and two for backstitch.

Trick or Treat?

This Hallowe'en card uses a fluorescent thread for a fun effect. You could stitch the motifs individually on badges or party items.

Quicker

Finished design size on 14-count 6.7 x 5cm (2½ x 2in)

You Will Need
- 18 x 13cm (7 x 5in) 14-count white Aida
- Double-fold card to fit embroidery

Stitch and make up your card – see Quick Stitch, page 5.

Quickest

Boo!

The little ghost is stitched using glow-in-the-dark white thread with fluorescent green backstitch.

Finished design size on 14-count 3.5 x 3.6cm (1⅜ x 1½in)

You Will Need
- 10 x 10cm (4 x 4in) 14-count black Aida
- Single-fold gift tag to fit embroidery
- Ribbon to trim • Bat confetti (HobbyCraft)

Follow Quick Stitch, page 5 but use three strands for cross stitch. Trim and mount on the tag. Tie the ribbon through the hole. To finish, glue on bat confetti.

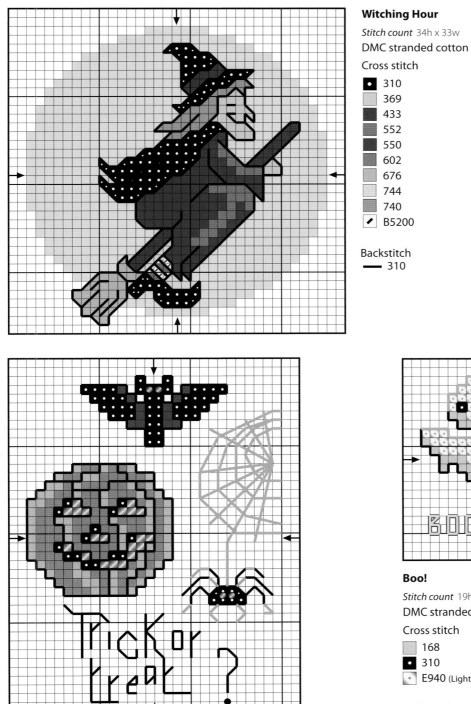

Witching Hour

Stitch count 34h x 33w

DMC stranded cotton

Cross stitch

■	310
▨	369
■	433
■	552
■	550
■	602
■	676
▨	744
■	740
✎	B5200

Backstitch

— 310

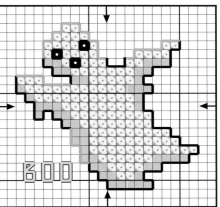

Boo!

Stitch count 19h x 20w

DMC stranded cotton

Cross stitch

▨	168
■	310
▨	E940 (Light Effects)

Backstitch

— 310

═══ E940 (Light Effects)

─── E990 (Light Effects)

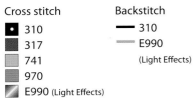

Trick or Treat?

Stitch count 37h x 28w

DMC stranded cotton

Cross stitch

■	310
■	317
▨	741
■	970
▨	E990 (Light Effects)

Backstitch

— 310

─── E990 (Light Effects)

French knots

● 310

◓ E990 (Light Effects)

Thanksgiving Celebration Designs by Joan Elliott

Give Thanks

Give thanks for all things as you gather with family and friends to celebrate this day of abundance on the fourth Thursday of November.

You Will Need
- 24 x 24cm (9½ x 9½in) 18-count Fiddler's Light Aida
- Double-fold card to fit embroidery
- Narrow ribbon to trim

Stitch and make up your card –
see Quick Stitch, page 5.

Finished design size on 18-count 11.8 x 11.8cm (4½ x 4½in)

Thankful Turkey

Thanksgiving dinner just wouldn't be the same without the turkey!

You Will Need
- 19 x 19cm (7½ x 7½in) 14-count Fiddler's Light Aida
- Double-fold card to fit embroidery
- Narrow ribbon to trim

Stitch and make up your card –
see Quick Stitch, page 5.

Finished design size on 14-count 6.7 x 6.7cm (2½ x 2½in)

Fruits of the Fall

Stitch this autumnal design for a Thanksgiving gift tag or for a November birthday.

You Will Need
- 17.8 x 17.8cm (7 x 7in) 14-count Fiddler's Light Aida
- Double-fold card/tag to fit embroidery
- Narrow ribbon to trim

Stitch and make up your tag –
see Quick Stitch, page 5.

Finished design size on 14-count 4.5 x 4.5cm (1¾ x 1¾in)

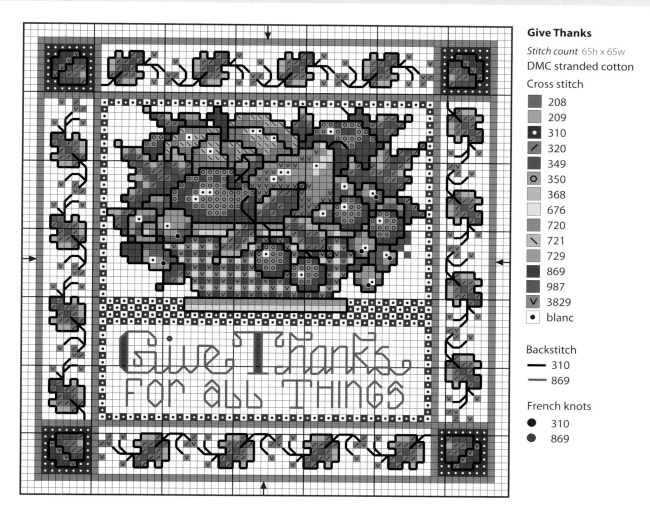

Give Thanks

Stitch count 65h x 65w

DMC stranded cotton

Cross stitch

- 208
- 209
- 310
- 320
- 349
- 350
- 368
- 676
- 720
- 721
- 729
- 869
- 987
- 3829
- blanc

Backstitch

— 310
— 869

French knots

- ● 310
- ● 869

Thankful Turkey

Stitch count 37h x 37w

DMC stranded cotton

Cross stitch

- 310
- 320
- 349
- 350
- 368
- 676
- 720
- 721
- 729
- 869
- 987
- 3829
- blanc

Backstitch

— 310

French knots

- ● 310

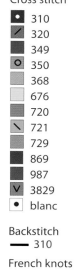

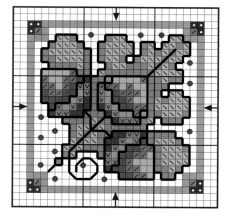

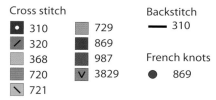

Fruits of the Fall

Stitch count 25h x 25w

DMC stranded cotton

Cross stitch

310		729	
320		869	
368		987	
720		3829	
721			

Backstitch

— 310

French knots

- ● 869

Oh, Holy Night   Designs by Lesley Teare

Finished design size on 14-count
14 x 3.3cm (5½ x 1¼in)

We Three Kings

Stitch three ornate crowns for a triple-aperture card and embellish the shiny metallic cross stitch with gold seed beads.

You Will Need
- 25.5 x 10cm (10 x 4in) 14-count pale blue Aida
- Mill Hill seed beads 00557 gold
- Double-fold card with triple aperture to fit embroidery (Impress Cards)
- Gold felt-tip pen

Stitch and make up your card – see Quick Stitch, page 5. Write 'We Three Kings' in gold on the card.

Away in a Manger

This traditional Christmas scene makes a charming greetings card.

You Will Need
- 12.7 x 10cm (5 x 4in) 14-count pale blue Aida
- Double-fold card with arched aperture to fit embroidery (Impress Cards)

Stitch and make up your card – see Quick Stitch, page 5. Use one strand for star stitches (page 95).

Finished design size on 14-count
6 x 4cm (2⅜ x 1½in)

Little Town of Bethlehem

A gold foil tag and metallic thread will turn the smallest Christmas gift into something really special.

You Will Need
- 10 x 10cm (4 x 4in) 14-count pale blue Aida
- Gold card for tag • Iron-on interfacing • Gold ribbon for tie

Follow Quick Stitch, page 5.
Make a tag from gold card (see page 98).

Finished design size on 14-count
2.5 x 3.3cm (1 x 1¼in)

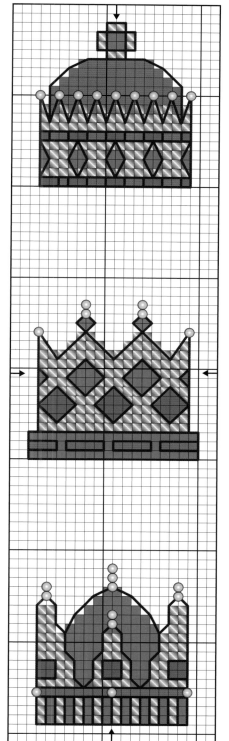

We Three Kings

Stitch count 77h x 18w

DMC stranded cotton

Cross stitch

- 349
- 702
- 3807
- Kreinik #4 braid 002 gold (use 1 strand)

Backstitch

—— 801

Mill Hill seed beads

- ○ 00557 gold

Away in a Manger

Stitch count 33h x 22w

DMC stranded cotton

Cross stitch

729	817	· 3865
744	792	Kreinik #4 braid 002 gold (use 1 strand)
801	3770	

Backstitch

—— 801

—— Kreinik #4 braid 002 gold (use 1 strand for star stitch)

Little Town of Bethlehem

Stitch count 15h x 18w

DMC stranded cotton

Cross stitch

- 677
- · 3865
- Kreinik #4 braid 002 gold (use 1 strand)

Backstitch

—— 167

—— Kreinik #4 braid 002 gold (use 1 strand for star stitch)

Let It Snow, Let It Snow, Let It Snow! Designs by Joanne Sanderson

Finished design size on 14-count
7.3 x 7.3cm (3 x 3in)

Quick

White Winter Bear

Stitch this cute polar bear in a weekend –
the perfect Christmas card for someone special.

You Will Need
- 15cm x 15cm (6 x 6in) 14-count white Aida
- Double-fold card to fit embroidery

Stitch and make up your card – see Quick Stitch, page 5.

Quicker

Jolly Santa

Santa's cheery face could also be
stitched on pale blue or Lurex Aida.

You Will Need
- 18 x 13cm (7 x 5in) 14-count navy Aida
- Double-fold card to fit embroidery
- Small piece of white card • Snowflake punch (HobbyCraft)

Follow Quick Stitch, page 5 but use three
strands for cross stitch. Decorate with snowflakes.

Finished design size on 14-count
5.6 x 5.6cm (2¼ x 2¼in)

Quickest

Rudolph's Ready!

This cute reindeer can also be stitched on
white Aida, using two strands for cross stitch.

You Will Need
- 10 x 10cm (4 x 4in) 14-count navy Aida
- Silver card for tag 18 x 7.6cm (7 x 3in) • Ribbon for tie

Follow Quick Stitch, page 5 but use three strands for cross stitch. Fold the
silver card in half. Punch a hole for the ribbon tie. Trim the
embroidery and mount on the tag.

Finished design size on
14-count
3 x 2.5cm (1¼ x 1in)

White Winter Bear

Stitch count 40h x 40w

DMC stranded cotton

Cross stitch

╲	168
╱	304
	352
	666
	726
	963
	972
	3756
	3761
	3799
	3838
•	B5200

Backstitch

— 666

— 3799

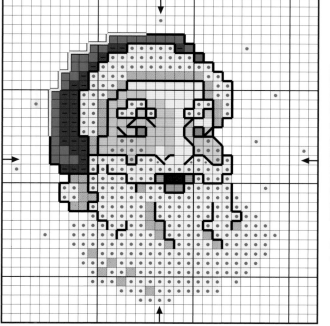

Jolly Santa

Stitch count 31h x 31w

DMC stranded cotton

Cross stitch

	310
	415
	666
	754
	816
	948
	961
•	3716
	3839
•	blanc

Backstitch

— 310

▭ blanc

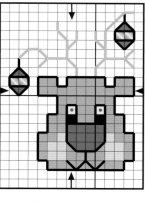

Rudolph's Ready!

Stitch count 17h x 13w

DMC stranded cotton

Cross stitch

	310		963
	666	•	blanc
	738	╲	E3825 (Light Effects)

Backstitch

— 310

— 738

Christmas Is For Giving Designs by Claire Crompton

Quick

Finished design size on 28-count
9 x 7.6cm (3½ x 3in)

Snow Fairy

Full of sparkle and merriment, the snow fairy scatters snowflakes wherever she goes.

You Will Need
- 18 x 18cm (7 x 7in) 28-count lilac evenweave
- Double-fold card to fit embroidery

Stitch and make up your card – see Quick Stitch, page 5. For tweeded threads, use one strand of each colour in the needle.

Quicker

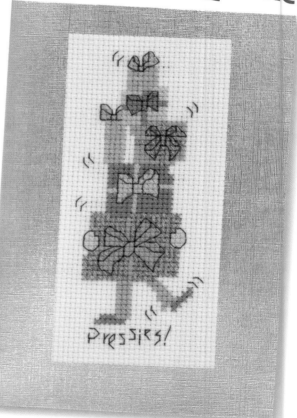

Pressies!

You can never have too many presents at Christmas time!

You Will Need
- 22 x 15cm (9 x 6in) 14-count white Aida
- Single-fold card to fit embroidery

Stitch and make up your card – see Quick Stitch, page 5. For tweeded threads, use one strand of each colour in the needle.

Finished design size on 14-count
11 x 4.8cm (4⅜ x 1⅝in)

Quickest

Finished design size on 14-count
4 x 4cm (1½ x 1½in)

Mistletoe Gift

With this little card there will always be mistletoe around when you need it!

You Will Need
- 10 x 10cm (4 x 4in) 16-count red Aida
- Single-fold card to fit embroidery

Follow Quick Stitch, page 5. Trim the embroidery and mount on the tag. Punch a hole for ribbon and write your message.

Snow Fairy

Stitch count 50h x 42w

DMC stranded cotton

Cross stitch

▨ 948

· B5200

▨ 3747 + E3747 (Light Effects)
(1 strand of each)

▨ B5200 + E5200 (Light Effects)
(1 strand of each)

Backstitch

—— 413

══ B5200 (2 strands)

French knots

● 413

○ B5200

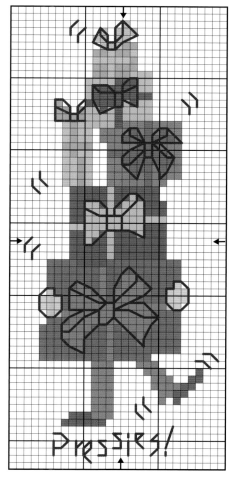

Pressies!

Stitch count 61h x 26w

DMC stranded cotton

Cross stitch

▨ 316

▨ 948

▨ 3752

▨ 3819

▨ 3825

▨ 155 + E211 (Light Effects)
(1 strand of each)

▨ 772 + E966 (Light Effects)
(1 strand of each)

▨ 3752 + E3747 (Light Effects)
(1 strand of each)

Backstitch

—— 3858

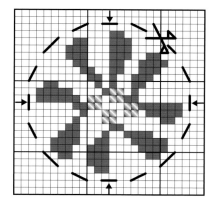

Mistletoe Gift

Stitch count 22h x 22w

DMC stranded cotton

Cross stitch

▨ 904

▨ E5200 (Light Effects)

Backstitch

—— 310

Materials and Techniques

This section describes the materials and equipment you need to make the cards in this book, followed by the basic techniques and stitches required. For beginners there are some handy tips on page 95 for perfect stitching.

Equipment

Very few materials and equipment are needed for successful cross stitch embroidery.

Fabrics

The fabrics used for counted cross stitch, mainly Aidas and evenweaves, are woven so they have the same number of threads or blocks to 2.5cm (1in) in both directions. They are available in different counts – the higher the count, the more threads or stitches to 2.5cm (1in), and the finer the fabric.

Aida This is ideal for the beginner because the threads are woven in blocks rather than singly. It is available in many fibres, colours and counts and as different width bands. When stitching on Aida, one block on the fabric corresponds to one square on a chart and generally cross stitch is worked over *one block*.

Evenweaves These are made from various fibres including linen, cotton and acrylic. Evenweaves are woven singly and are available in different colours, counts and bands. To even out any oddities in the weave, cross stitch is usually worked over *two threads* of evenweave fabric.

Threads

The most commonly used thread for counted embroidery is stranded cotton (floss). The DMC range has been used by the designers in this book but if you prefer to work with the Anchor range ask at your local craft shop for a conversion table.

Some of the card designs feature metallic threads to create extra sparkle. The new Light Effects range from DMC that has been used on many of the cards has 36 colours with different effects – jewel, metal, antique, pearlescent and fluorescent. These can be used alone or combined with stranded cottons. Kreinik metallic braid #4 features on many cards and creates a lovely gleam. Caron space-dyed threads have also been used to provide subtle variegated shades. The project instructions give how many strands of each thread to use.

Tweeding You can increase the number of thread colours in your palette by blending or tweeding – that is, combining two or more thread colours in your needle at the same time and working as one to achieve a mottled effect.

Beads

Some of the card designs use Mill Hill glass seed beads to bring an extra sparkle to the cross stitch. If you want to use beads as an embellishment there are many types and colours to choose from (see Suppliers). See page 95 for how to attach beads.

Tools

There are many tools and gadgets available for embroidery in craft shops but you really only need the following.

Needles Use blunt tapestry needles for counted cross stitch. The most common sizes used are 24 and 26 but the size depends on the project you are working on and personal preference. Avoid leaving a needle in the fabric unless it is gold plated or it may cause marks. A beading needle (or fine 'sharp' needle), which is much thinner, will be needed to attach beads.

Scissors Use dressmaker's shears for cutting fabric and a small, sharp pair of pointed scissors for cutting embroidery threads.

Frames and hoops These are not essential, especially for the small designs in this book but if you do choose to use one, select one large enough to hold the complete design to avoid marking the fabric and flattening stitches.

Cards

Most of the cards in this book have been mounted into double-fold cards with an aperture or on the front of single-fold windowless cards. See page 96 for using ready-made card blanks, page 98 for making your own cards and page 100 for ideas on adding trims and embellishments.

Basic Techniques

This section describes the techniques you need to prepare fabric for work, use the charts and keys, and work the stitches.

Preparing Fabric for Work

Preparing your fabric for work takes a little time but is worth it for a superior result.

- Press embroidery fabric before stitching and trim the selvedge or rough edges.
- Work from the middle of the fabric and middle of the chart to ensure your design is centred on the fabric.
- Find the middle of the fabric by folding in four and pressing lightly. Mark the folds with tailor's chalk or tacking (basting) following a fabric thread. When working with linen sew a narrow hem around all raw edges to preserve them.

Stitch Count and Design Size

Each project gives details of the stitch count and finished design size but if you wish to work the design on a different count fabric you will need to re-calculate the finished size. Count the number of stitches in the design and divide this by the fabric count number, e.g., 56 stitches x 56 stitches ÷ by 14-count = a design size of 4 x 4in (10 x 10cm). Remember, working on evenweave usually means stitching over two threads not one, so divide the fabric count by two before you start.

Starting and Finishing Stitching

Unless indicated otherwise, begin stitching in the middle of a design to ensure an adequate margin for making up. Start and finish stitching neatly, avoiding knots which create lumps.

Knotless loop start This neat start can be used with an even number of strands i.e., 2, 4 or 6.

To stitch with two strands, begin with one strand about 80cm (30in). Double it and thread the needle with the two ends. Put the needle up through the fabric from the wrong side, where you intend to begin stitching, leaving the loop at the back. Form a half cross stitch, put the needle back through the fabric and through the waiting loop. The stitch is now anchored and you can begin.

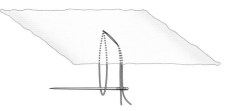

A knotless loop start

Using the Charts

The designs in this book are worked from colour charts, with symbols where necessary. Each square, both occupied and unoccupied, represents one block of Aida (or two threads of linen). Each occupied square equals one stitch. Three-quarter cross stitches are shown as a triangle within a grid square. Some designs use French knots and beads, and these are labelled in the chart keys.

Away waste knot start Start this way if using an odd number of strands or when tweeding threads.

Thread your needle with the number of strands required and knot the end. Insert the needle into the right side of the fabric some way away from where you wish to begin stitching. Stitch towards the knot and cut it off when the threads are anchored. Alternatively, snip off the knot, thread the needle and work under a few stitches to anchor.

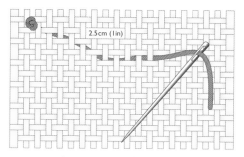

2.5cm (1in)

An away waste knot start

Finishing stitching At the back of the work, pass the needle and thread under several stitches of the same or similar colour, and then snip off the loose end close to the stitching. You can begin a new colour in a similar way.

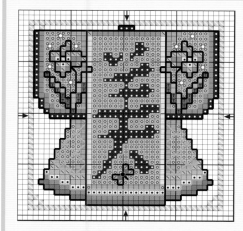

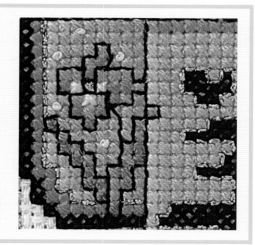

Working the Stitches

The cards in the book use basic stitches that are easy to work: simply follow the instructions and diagrams here.

Cross Stitch

This is the most commonly used stitch in this book and it can be worked singly or in two journeys. For neat stitching, keep the top stitch facing the same direction. Half cross stitch is simply a single diagonal line.

Cross stitch on Aida Cross stitch on Aida fabric is normally worked over one block of the fabric.

To work a complete cross stitch, follow the numbered sequence in the diagram below: bring the needle up through the fabric at 1, cross one block of the fabric and insert the needle at 2. Push the needle through and bring it up at 3, ready to complete the stitch at 4. To work the adjacent stitch, bring the needle up at the bottom right-hand corner of the first stitch.

Single cross stitch on Aida fabric

To work cross stitches in two journeys, work the first leg of the cross stitch as above but instead of completing the stitch, work the adjacent half stitch and continue on to the end of the row. Complete all the crosses by working the other diagonals on the return journey.

Cross stitch worked in two journeys on Aida

Cross stitch on evenweave

Cross stitch on evenweave is usually worked over two threads of the fabric in each direction to even out any oddities in the thickness of the fibres. Bring the needle up to the left of a vertical thread to make it easier to spot counting mistakes. If you are working your cross stitch in two journeys, use a sewing movement, half cross stitch in one direction and then work back and cover the original stitches with the second row. This forms neat, single vertical lines on the back and gives somewhere to finish off raw ends.

Single cross stitch on evenweave

Three-quarter Cross Stitch

Three-quarter cross stitch is a fractional stitch which can produce the illusion of curves. The stitch can be formed on either Aida or evenweave but is easier and more successful on evenweave. Three-quarter cross stitches are shown on charts as a triangle (half square).

Work the first half of a cross stitch as usual. Work the second 'quarter' stitch over the top and down into the central hole to anchor the first half of the stitch. If using Aida, you will need to push the needle through the centre of a block of the fabric. Where two three-quarter stitches lie back-to-back in the space of one full cross stitch, work both of the respective quarter stitches into the central hole.

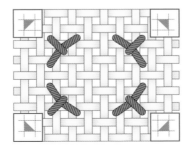

Three-quarter cross stitches on evenweave

Backstitch

Backstitch is used for outlining a design or part of a design, to add detail or emphasis, or for letters and numbers. It is added after the cross stitch has been completed so the backstitch line isn't broken by cross stitches. It is shown on charts by solid coloured lines.

Follow the numbered sequence in the diagram below, working the stitches over one block of Aida or two threads of even-weave, unless stated otherwise.

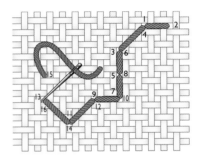

Backstitch

French Knot

French knots are small but important little stitches, which are predominantly used for eyes and to add detail to a design. They are shown on the charts as coloured circles, with the thread code in the key.

Bring the needle through to the front of the fabric and wind the thread around the needle twice. Begin to push the needle partly through to the back, one thread or part of a block away from the entry point (to stop the stitch being pulled to the wrong side). Gently pull the thread you have wound so it sits snugly at the point where the needle enters the fabric. Pull the needle through to the back and you should have a perfect knot in position. For bigger knots, it is best to add more strands of thread to the needle rather than winding more times.

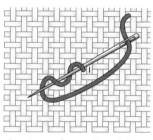

Starting to form a French knot

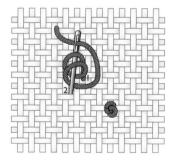

Completing a French knot

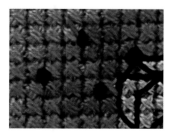

Long Stitch

Long straight stitches are used in some of the designs. They are very simple to stitch and can be worked on any fabric. To work long stitch, simply bring the needle and thread up where the stitch is to start, at 1 in the diagram below, and down where the chart indicates it should finish, at 2.

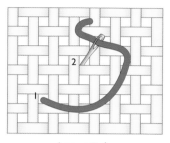

Long stitch

Star Stitch

Some designs use long stitches to create a little star. You could also use double cross stitch – see diagram below for working.

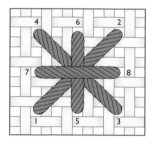

Star stitch (double cross stitch)

Adding Beads

Beads make a wonderful embellishment to cross stitch and are very effective on cards, especially small seed beads. Beads are shown on the charts as a large coloured circle, with details of the bead type, colour and code in the key. Attach beads using a beading needle or very fine 'sharp' needle, thread that matches the bead colour and a half cross stitch (or full cross stitch).

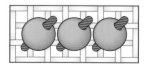

Attaching beads

Perfect Stitching

The following tips will not only help you produce beautiful stitching but also save you time.

Organize your threads before you start a project as this will help to save time by avoiding confusion later. Put threads on an organizer (available from craft shops) and always include the manufacturer's name and the shade number.

For a smooth finish, separate the strands on a skein of stranded cotton (floss) before taking the number you need, realigning them and threading your needle.

To save time changing thread colours, work with several needles, each one threaded with a different colour.

When stitching with metallic threads, work with shorter lengths, about 30cm (12in) to avoid tangling and excessive wear on the thread.

If using a frame, try to avoid a hoop as it will stretch the fabric and leave a mark that may be difficult to remove later.

For neat cross stitch work the top stitches all facing the same direction.

When adding a backstitch outline, always add it after the cross stitch has been completed to prevent the solid line being broken.

Using Cards

Card and gift tag blanks to display your cross stitch embroidery are available in many types, shapes and sizes and of course rainbow colours. Your local craft store will stock some and there are many mail-order suppliers – see the list on page 103. If you send for a catalogue from a card blank manufacturer you will see what a huge range is available. There are cards with specialized finishes, with straight or decorative edges and with windows (apertures) in all shapes and sizes.

You can, of course, make your own cards and tags – see overleaf for basic instructions and also the Quick Card panel on page 101, which gives lots of handy hints and tips on creating and using cards for cross stitch embroidery.

The types of cards used
in this book are:

single-fold cards without aperture

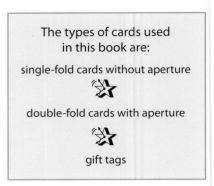

double-fold cards with aperture

gift tags

Mounting Embroidery on a Single-Fold Card without Aperture

This is simply a piece of card folded in half. Your cross stitch embroidery is attached to the front of the card with craft glue or double-sided tape. The edges of the embroidery could be frayed before it is stuck to the card or covered with a pretty trim.

1 First, make your embroidery more rigid and prevent the edges from fraying by backing it with iron-on interfacing (see opposite). If you want a fringe or frayed edges around the embroidery, iron-on a smaller piece of interfacing, to allow two or three rows of threads to be teased away before the card is mounted.

2 Trim the embroidery to the required size, making sure it looks straight on the card front. Apply strips of double-sided tape to the back of the embroidery and stick your embroidery on to the card in the position you've decided upon – this may be centrally or offset to either the top or bottom of the card (see the box on page 99 for ideas).

3 For a lovely finishing touch, edge the embroidery with a decorative trim (see Using Trims and Embellishments on pages 100/101). You could experiment with using double mounts (see box, left) and with the position of your design (see box page 99).

Using double mounts

Adding an extra mount or even two displays your cross stitch beautifully. Try using plain card that tones or contrasts with the design, or stick decorative paper to a piece of card first. You could also rotate the mount. See page 99 for positioning motifs.

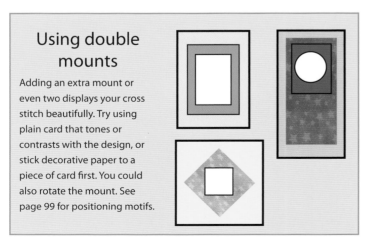

Mounting Embroidery in a Double-Fold Card with Aperture

This type of card consists of a piece of card folded into three sections, with the front section having a window or aperture to display your cross stitch design. The front section is then stuck to the middle part, thus hiding the back of the embroidery.

1 Lay the card right side up on top of the design so the stitching is in the middle of the aperture. Place a pin in each corner to mark where the aperture is, and then remove the card. Trim the embroidery so it fits behind the aperture with a border of about 2cm (¾in).

2 On the wrong side of the card, stick double-sided tape around the aperture and peel off the backing tape. (Note: cards from some manufacturers already have this tape in place.) Place the card over the design, using the pins to guide it into position. Press down firmly so the fabric is stuck securely to the card.

3 On the wrong side of the card, stick more double-sided tape around the edge of the middle section. Peel off the backing tape and fold the left section in to cover the back of the stitching, pressing down firmly.

You can create an attractive padded look by adding a piece of wadding (batting) to the back of the embroidery before you stick it to the card.

Mounting Embroidery on a Gift Tag

Gift tags are usually a single piece of card with the embroidery mounted on the front but they can also be a small single-fold or double-fold card. Gift tags are perfect for a quick-stitch project and turn even the simplest gift into something really special. There are a huge range of small motifs in the book specially designed for tags and small cards. These are easily stitched in a few hours and are excellent for using up spare pieces of embroidery fabric and leftover threads.

Mount your embroidery on a tag using iron-on interfacing to stiffen it (see below), in the same way as for a single-fold card without aperture. If your tag is a small double-fold card, mount your embroidery in the same way as described, left.

You can change the look of your gift tags in various ways – try cutting a decorative or deckle edge to the card, or fraying the edges of the embroidery or mounting the embroidery on a different coloured piece of card as a double mount (see bottom of page 96).

Using iron-on interfacing

Backing an embroidery with iron-on interfacing will stiffen it and provide a firm edge that can be trimmed neatly and will not fray easily. Place the embroidery face down on a soft towel and iron a piece of interfacing on the back using a medium iron (refer to the manufacturer's instructions). Some interfacings have a backing paper, which can be ironed on, if not use a pressing cloth.

If you want your embroidery to have a frayed edge or a fringe, cut the interfacing a little smaller than the embroidery. Iron it on the back centrally and this will leave some threads free around the edge, ready to be teased away.

Making Cards

There are so many types of card stock and decorative papers now available, in so many colours and finishes that you are sure to be tempted to make your own cards. Most craft stores also stock trims and embellishment galore and you will have no difficulty finding that extra something to complement your cross stitch perfectly. See the Quick Card panel on page 101 for some ideas on producing cards quickly.

To Make Your Own Cards
You Will Need
Card stock • Craft knife • Cutting mat • Pencil and ruler
• Sharp scissors • Double-sided tape or other adhesive • Tweezers
• Bone folder (optional) • Trims and embellishments (optional)

To Make a Single-Fold Card without Aperture

This is the simplest type of card to make, perfect for those occasions when there's little time. For layout ideas, see positioning motifs, opposite.

1 Choose a card colour to complement your embroidery and thick enough to stand once the embroidery is attached. Cut a piece large enough to house your finished embroidery on one half.

2 Fold the card into two and crease the fold line firmly (easy to do with a bone folder, if not, use the back of a craft knife. The card is now ready for you to mount the embroidery on to the front (see page 96).

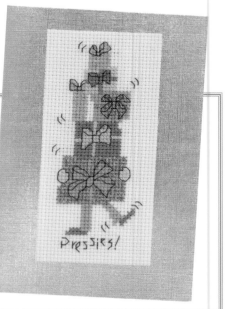

To Make a Gift Tag

Tags can be bought ready-made but they are so easy to make yourself. The following instructions are for a simple tag but you could also make a tag like a small single-fold card (see above).

1 For a basic tag, choose a card colour to complement your cross stitch and cut a piece of card a little larger than your finished design. Try using some decorative scissors, which cut an attractive deckle or patterned edge.

2 Mount your stitching on to the front of the tag with double-sided tape, backing it first with iron-on interfacing, as described on page 97.

3 Carefully punch a hole in the top corner of the tag and thread a piece of ribbon, raffia or decorative braid through to attach the tag to your gift.

4 Finally, write your message on the back of the tag. Experiment with different colours and types of pens. For example, metallic calligraphy pens give the simplest tag design a really special look, while brightly coloured gel pens are ideal for a fun and funky finish on tags for children and teenagers.

To Make a Double-Fold Card with Aperture

The size of card you make will depend on personal preference and the cross stitch design you wish to display. The instructions below describe a simple card but the measurements given can easily be changed.

1 Start with an A4 sized piece of card, 29.5 x 21cm (11¾ x 8¼in), in a colour to complement your embroidery. On the wrong side of the card, draw two faint pencil lines dividing it into three equal sections of 9.8cm (3⅞in), as shown in the diagram below. Score gently along each line with a bone folder or the back of a craft knife to make folding easier.

2 In the centre section, mark an aperture as shown in the diagram or one slightly smaller than the finished size of your cross stitch design, leaving a border around the edge – in this case 2.5cm (1in) at the top and bottom and 1.25cm (½in) at either side.

3 Cut out the aperture with a sharp craft knife, carefully cutting into the corners neatly. Trim the left edge of the first section by 2mm (⅛in) so that it lies flat when folded over to the inside of the card. This will cover the back of the stitching. Fold the left and then the right section on the scored lines. Your card is now ready for your embroidery – see page 97 for mounting.

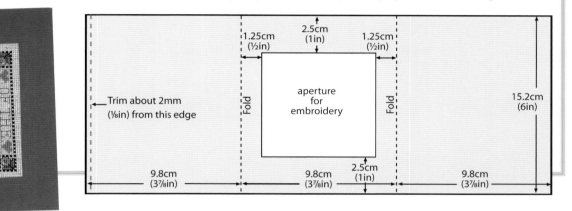

To Make a Badge

Many of the smaller designs would make great badges, to wear on clothing or to attach to cards.

1 Iron two layers of interfacing (see page 97) on the back of the finished embroidery, one layer a time, to make it rigid.

2 Cut a piece of felt the same size as the embroidery and sew a brooch pin or safety pin into the middle. Iron a piece of double-sided interfacing on to the front of the felt. Peel off the backing paper, place the felt on the back of the embroidery, pin outwards, and iron the layers to fuse everything together.

3 Trim the embroidery to size and shape. If attaching to a card, pierce two holes in the card for the pin.

Positioning motifs

You will find that even the simplest cross stitch motif takes on a new dimension if placed in different positions on the front of a card. Motifs can also be repeated and arranged in rows or groups. Try applying the 'rule of thirds', where the card face is divided into thirds by imaginary lines, either vertically or horizontally, with your design occupying one of the thirds. Why not experiment with some of the layout examples shown below? See page 96 for using mounts.

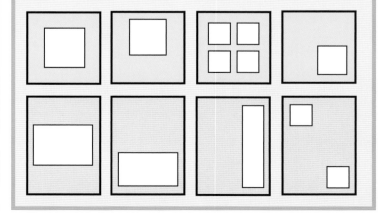

Adding Trims and Embellishments

A handmade card displaying your cross stitch will look even more special with the addition of a pretty trim or embellishment. Some trims have an adhesive backing, others can be glued into place with craft glue, a hot glue gun or narrow double-sided tape. There are so many gorgeous embellishments to choose from – sometimes all that is needed for a charming finishing touch is a simple gauze or satin ribbon in a toning or contrasting colour. Here are some other suggestions.

Look for unusual trims, which can be used as a framing feature or cut up into smaller motifs to embellish the corners of a design

Collect card stock and decorative papers – ideas for cards will flow when you are faced with a delicious selection

Decorative trims

These can include ribbon, braid, raffia, cord and feathers and are ideal for edging cross stitch designs, framing your work beautifully or they can be used as trims and bows to embellish the card itself.

Rubber stamps

Craft stores are crammed with rubber stamps of all shapes and sizes. Use them to decorate your cards, inside and out, using ink stamp colours to tone with the cross stitch design.

Paper punches

These little gadgets punch out paper shapes, which can add an interesting finishing touch – see the snowflakes on the card on page 88. Punches are available in many different sizes, shapes and themes.

Try gauzy metallic ribbons for decorative bows or stylish borders for your cards

Don't forget gorgeous pearls and beads for a gleaming, three-dimensional look

Toppers

There are hundreds of these little pre-made decorations available, made from all sorts of materials and in many shapes, including stars, hearts, flowers and sequins. They often have an adhesive backing and can be used to give a three-dimensional effect to enhance your cross stitch and give your cards a really stylish handmade look.

Outline stickers

These are self-adhesive labels that you can use to embellish your cards. There are letters, numbers, greeting phrases, borders – literally thousands of motifs to choose from.

Rub-ons

These are dry transfers called decals that are applied to paper and card by rubbing – great for adding names, dates and sentiments and for other decorative elements, such as borders and scrolls.

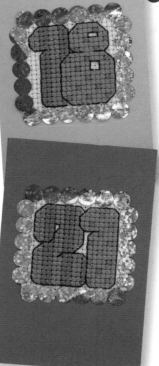

Decorative pens

There are many types of pens available for adding a personal touch to your cards, maybe in the form of a message or to complement the cross stitch by adding a frame around the design or little drawings and motifs, such as the paw prints on the card above. Try using gold and silver calligraphy pens for an extra special look.

Quick Cards

And finally, here are some handy hints on producing cross stitch cards quickly and easily.

Find a large box to store your basic card-making accessories in and then you will always be able to find what you need at a moment's notice. Keep the following items in the box: sharp scissors, craft knife, small cutting mat, double-sided adhesive tape, tweezers, pencil and ruler

Keep some ready-made card blanks in neutral colours such as white, cream, grey and ivory as these will tone with many different cross stitch designs.

Keep some off-cuts of Aida fabric in pale or neutral colours so you always have some to hand for a quick cross stitch session.

Have a selection of sheets of card handy, in various colours and finishes, so you can quickly make up a card.

Cut some templates from thick card or plastic to use for card apertures – squares, oblongs and circles of different sizes are the most useful – then simply draw around the shape instead of measuring the window each time.

Keep a selection of narrow ribbons and trims to quickly add an embellishment to a card. You could also have a small collection of ribbon bows or other toppers in neutral colours that will tone with most cross stitch designs.

Store some felt-tip pens for writing messages on cards and adding decorations. Keep a silver and gold calligraphy marker for a more decorative look.

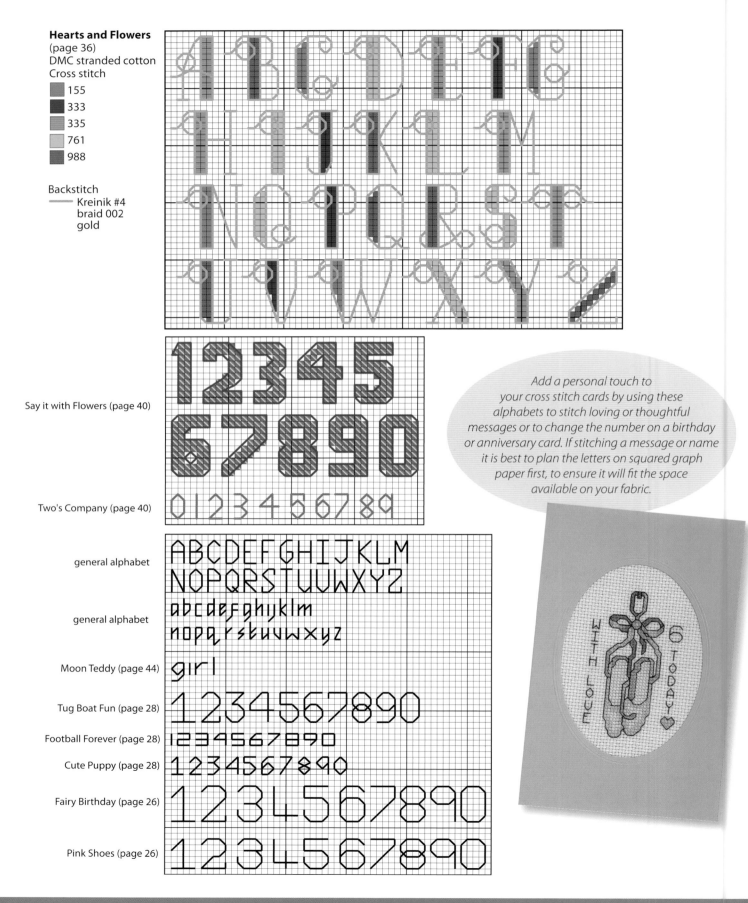

Hearts and Flowers
(page 36)
DMC stranded cotton
Cross stitch

- 155
- 333
- 335
- 761
- 988

Backstitch
— Kreinik #4
braid 002
gold

Say it with Flowers (page 40)

Two's Company (page 40)

general alphabet

general alphabet

Moon Teddy (page 44)

Tug Boat Fun (page 28)

Football Forever (page 28)

Cute Puppy (page 28)

Fairy Birthday (page 26)

Pink Shoes (page 26)

Add a personal touch to your cross stitch cards by using these alphabets to stitch loving or thoughtful messages or to change the number on a birthday or anniversary card. If stitching a message or name it is best to plan the letters on squared graph paper first, to ensure it will fit the space available on your fabric.

Suppliers

The following suppliers will have the materials and equipment you need to create the cross stitch cards in this book. Two card blank manufacturers were used for all the card mounts: Craft Creations and Impress Cards – see contact details below for catalogues.

UK

Coats Crafts UK
PO Box 22, Lingfield Estate, McMullen Road, Darlington, County Durham DL1 1YQ, UK
tel: 01325 365457 (for a list of stockists)
For Anchor stranded cotton (floss)
and other embroidery supplies

Craft Creations Limited
1C Ingersoll House, Delamare Road, Cheshunt, Herts EN8 9HD
tel: 019992 781900
www.craftcreations.com
For greetings card blanks
and card-making accessories

DMC Creative World
Pullman Road, Wigston, Leicestershire LE18 2DY, UK
tel: 0116 281 1040
fax: 0116 281 3592
www.dmc/cw.com
For a huge range of threads, fabrics
and needlework supplies

Framecraft Miniatures Ltd
Unit 3, Isis House, Lindon Road, Brownhills, West Midlands WS8 7BW
tel/fax (UK): 01543 360842
tel (international): 44 1543 453154
email: sales@framecraft.com
www.framecraft.com
For Mill Hill beads, buttons, and many other
pre-finished items with cross stitch inserts

Impress Cards & Craft Materials
Slough Farm, Westhall, Suffolk IP19 8RN
tel: 01986 781422
email: sales@impresscards.co.uk
www.impresscards.com
For ready-made card blanks and craft materials

HobbyCraft Superstores
Help Desk, The Peel Centre, St Ann Way, Gloucester, Gloucestershire GL1 5SF
tel: 01452 424999
www.hobbycraft.co.uk
For a huge range of craft supplies
(stores throughout the UK)

Memory Keepsakes
Shakeford Mill, Hinstock, Market Drayton, Shropshire TF9 2SP
tel: 01630 638342
email: sales@memorykeepsakes.co.uk
www.memorykeepsakes.co.uk
For cardmaking supplies

Paper Cellar
Parkville House, Red Lion Parade, Pinner, Middlesex HA5 3RR
tel: 0871 8713711
email: contact@papercellar.com
www.papercellar.com
For paper and cardmaking supplies

V V Rouleaux
54 Sloane Square, London SW1W 8AX
tel: 0207 730 3125
email: general@vvrouleaux.com
www.vvrouleaux.com
For ribbons and bead trims

Willow Fabrics
95 Town Lane, Mobberley, Knutsford, Cheshire WA16 7HH
tel freephone (UK): 0800 0567811
(elsewhere): #44 (0) 1565 87 2225
www.willowfabrics.com
For embroidery fabrics and Madeira threads

USA

Charles Craft Inc
PO Box 1049, Laurenburg, NC 28353, USA
tel: 910 844 3521
email: ccraft@carolina.net
www.charlescraft.com
Cross stitch fabrics and accessories

Kreinik Manufacturing Company Inc
3106 Timanus Lane, Suite 101, Baltimore, MD 21244
tel: 1800 537 2166
email: kreinik@kreinik.com
www.kreinik.com
For a wide range of metallic threads and
blending filaments

Mill Hill, a division of Wichelt Imports Inc.
N162 Hwy 35, Stoddard WI 54658
tel: 608 788 4600
fax: 608 788 6040
email: millhill@millhill.com
www. millhill.com
For Mill Hill beads and a US source for
Framecraft products

Zweigart/Joan Toggit Ltd
262 Old Brunswick Road, Suite E, Piscataway, NJ 08854-3756, USA
tel: 732 562 8888
email: info@zweigart.com
www.zweigart.com
For cross stitch fabrics and accessories

Acknowledgments

The publishers would like to thank the following people for their contributions: Claire Crompton, Joan Elliott, Joanne Sanderson and Lesley Teare.

Additional thanks go to Lin Clements for project managing this title, writing and editing text and preparing the charts, and to Karl Adamson and Kim Sayer for the photography.

Claire Crompton wishes to thank DMC Creative World for supplying embroidery fabrics, stranded cottons and Light Effects threads.

The Designers

Claire Crompton

Claire studied knitwear design at college before joining the design team at DMC, and finally going freelance. Claire's work has appeared in several magazines, including *Cross Stitch Magic*. Her designs also feature in many David & Charles books including, *Cross Stitch Greetings Cards*, *Cross Stitch Alphabets*, *Cross Stitch Angels*, *Cross Stitch Fairies*, *Magical Cross Stitch* and in her new book *Cross Stitch Card Collection*. Claire lives in the Tamar valley, Cornwall.

Joanne Sanderson

Joanne started designing cross stitch when a friend asked her to produce a chart. Soon after she won a design competition in the *World of Cross Stitch* magazine and has been designing ever since. She now contributes to many needlecraft magazines including *Cross Stitcher*, *Cross Stitch Collection* and *Quick & Easy Cross Stitch* and produces designs for DMC kits. Joanne lives in Yorkshire, UK, with her husband and daughter.

Joan Elliott

Joan's creations have been enchanting cross stitch enthusiasts the world over for years and she is a leading artist for Design Works Crafts Inc. Her debut book for David & Charles, *A Cross Stitcher's Oriental Odyssey* was followed by *Cross Stitch Teddies*, *Cross Stitch Sentiments and Sayings* and *Native American Cross Stitch*. She is currently working on her next book. Joan divides her time between New York and Vermont.

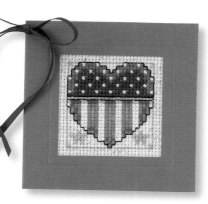

Lesley Teare

Lesley trained as a textile designer, with a degree in printed and woven textiles. For some years she has been one of DMC's leading designers and her designs also feature in many cross stitch magazines. Lesley has contributed to five books for David & Charles: *Cross Stitch Greetings Cards*, *Cross Stitch Alphabets*, *Cross Stitch Angels*, *Cross Stitch Fairies* and *Magical Cross Stitch*. Her first solo book for David & Charles was *101 Weekend Cross Stitch Gifts*, followed by *Travel the World in Cross Stitch*. Lesley lives in Hitcham, Suffolk.

Index